A HISTORY OF
Ireland

A HISTORY OF Ireland

Culture, Art, Landscape and Architecture

Dominic Connolly

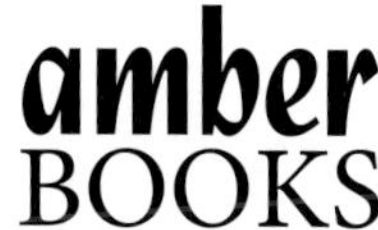

First published in 2025

Published by Amber Books Ltd
United House
London N7 9DP
United Kingdom
www.amberbooks.co.uk
Facebook: amberbooks
YouTube: amberbooksltd
Instagram: amberbooksltd
X(Twitter): @amberbooks

ISBN: 978-1-83886-614-3

Editor: Michael Spilling
Designer: Mark Batley
Picture research: Adam Gnych

Printed in China

Contents

PRE-CHRISTIAN IRELAND

Given that Ireland has had such an effect on the world – especially in the spread of Christianity and in populating America and Australasia – it is ironic that it was one of the last places in Europe to be populated by humans.

There is evidence that – before sea levels rose to cut off Ireland from Britain as well as from the rest of Europe – 33,000 years ago hunter-gatherers followed reindeer herds around the land mass of what is now Ireland. But a more consistent record of Ireland being populated starts around only 12,500 years ago.

ICE AGE

Between those periods, the whole of Ireland was scoured by huge ice sheets, during the last glacial maximum of 26,000 to 20,000 years ago. When they retreated, they temporarily left an ice bridge between Ireland and Scotland, but for the past 14,000 years Ireland has been separated by sea from Britain. For this reason, there are a number of temperate species that abound in England, Wales and Scotland – as well as in continental Europe – that are not native to Ireland. Snakes and lizards are an example – it was just too cold for them to spread to Ireland when it was linked to mainland Britain in the dying days of glaciation.

Similarly, it is most likely that the people who settled in Ireland could only have arrived by boats. And their familiarity with water continued, with subsequent inland communities usually building up close to water.

EARLY SETTLERS

The earliest settlers – hunter-gatherers – would have lived in shelters of animal skins or thatch spread over wooden frames, and would have numbered no more than a few thousand over the whole of Ireland.

OPPOSITE:
BELTANY STONE CIRCLE
This circle from the Bronze Age sits in County Donegal and many of the original stones were taken from the site and used for homesteads and field boundaries. The site's name may be related to the Celtic fertility festival in May, Beltane.

STRAITS OF MOYLE

The Straits of Moyle – otherwise known as the North Channel – separate Ireland and Scotland, and it is thought that there was an ice bridge between the two during the last glaciation, allowing animals from Britain to populate Ireland.

ABOVE:
CÉIDE FIELDS
County Mayo's Céide Fields is the oldest known field system in the world. Barley and wheat were grown here, and the system was preserved under peat bog for centuries. The area would have originally been covered by trees such as pine and birch.

LEFT:
STONE AGE SETTLEMENT
A re-creation of a Stone Age settlement at the Irish National Heritage Park in County Wexford. The earliest evidence of human settlement in Ireland dates to around 7000 BCE, after the ice bridge connecting Ireland and Britain had melted.

OPPOSITE:
RED DEER
Red deer arrived in Ireland around the end of the last Ice Age and have been a continuous presence since, although their populations have suffered because of deforestation and over-hunting.

Domestication of animals spread across Europe and reached Ireland with cattle being brought by boat into the north around 4300 BCE, along with red deer. Meanwhile, knowledge of how to cultivate cereals was also making its way into Ireland from the continent, as is shown by the Ceide Fields in County Mayo. This field system – the oldest known one in the world – was preserved by peat bog for centuries. Wheat and barley were the principal crops. Pottery also made its appearance in Ireland around this time.

STONE MONUMENTS

With populations settling into permanent communities based around fields – and flocks and herds of animals – the numbers of people in Ireland boomed. And those people left their mark in the many megalithic monuments that still exist around Ireland.

The largest of these are tombs, and there are known to be 1200 of them in Ireland. Early communities also left elaborate rock art – grooves carved into open-air stone – often called Atlantic Rock Art because of its similarity to engravings found along much of the west coast of Europe.

ABOVE & PREVIOUS PAGES:
LABBACALLEE CAIRN BURIAL WEDGE TOMB
The tomb at Labbacallee in County Cork – dating from around 2300 BCE – is the largest wedge tomb in Ireland. Wedge tombs are so named because their burial chambers were narrower at one end than the other. These tombs generally face west, towards the setting sun.

OPPOSITE:
JADEITITE AXEHEAD
This axehead – found in Donegal and dating from 4000–3800 BCE – is evidence of an early trading culture in Ireland. The jadeitite originates from northern Italy and the stone was highly prized for its robust nature and green flecks.

RIGHT:
ARDGROOM STONE CIRCLE
This is one of the stones at the Ardgroom Stone Circle on the Beara Peninsula in County Cork. Nine of the 11 stones are still standing – where they overlook a large area – and date from around 3000 BCE.

NEWGRANGE PASSAGE TOMB
Newgrange Passage Tomb overlooks the River Boyne in County Meath and, dating to around 3200 BCE, is older than Stonehenge and the Egyptian Pyramids. It is part of the Brú na Bóinne tomb complex.

Further immigration into Ireland brought knowledge of how to use metal to create drinking vessels and axe heads. Swords, daggers and hatchets were subsequently produced, and the Irish specialized in a horn-shaped trumpet. The bronze used was made from the copper found in the southwest of Ireland and tin brought in from Cornwall.

BRONZE AGE HOARDS

Ireland was also rich in gold, and more Bronze Age gold hoards have been discovered here than anywhere else in Europe. Irish gold contributed to a flourishing of ornament creation, and gold items from Bronze Age Ireland were also exported and have been found as far away as Germany and Scandinavia.

Many Irish of the time lived in crannogs – which were also popular in Scotland. These were covered wooden structures built over shallow water, and many families and their animals would live there. The settlements offered security as well as access to fresh water, and the geography of Ireland, with its many rivers and lakes, lent itself to them, as it also did in Scotland.

HILL OF TARA

The early Irish also settled in protected settlements such as ringforts and promontory forts. The ringforts might be small enough to house just some livestock, or could be large enough for several families.

During this period, the Hill of Tara grew in significance – although it was to become more revered later in the mythology that built up around it. The hill, in County Meath, boasted a number of ringforts and came to be seen as the inauguration place for the high kings of Ireland.

Another major hilltop site was Navan Fort – near Armagh, in Northern Ireland – which had a large circular building on top of it, built around 100 BCE.

More lasting evidence from this era that the people who had settled in Ireland were working together en masse are the earthworks at Black Pig's Dyke and Cliadh Dubh, which probably represented boundaries.

There are also toghers – wooden trackways across boggy areas – such as the Corlea Trackway in County Longford, from 148–147 BCE.

'BOG BODIES'

Peat bogs, crossed by such roads, are characteristic of Ireland, so it seems appropriate that they should have yielded so much evidence that tells us about Ireland's early days. More than a dozen 'bog bodies' have been found, some of which are skeletons, but in other cases the peat has preserved the flesh, hair and even clothing of those who had been buried.

Most of these now lie in Ireland's museums, and the history of how they have been collected and displayed reflects the story of Ireland. The British Museum housed a collection of antiquities when Ireland was under British rule, but as Ireland grew more confident, institutions there sprung up to house them, starting with Dublin's Royal Irish Academy in 1785.

FIRST WRITTEN RECORDS

The first written records of Celtic languages, from the fifth century, show that the people of Ireland were speaking an early form of Gaelic, related but different to the Brittonic that was being spoken in western Britain, Brittany and Spain's Galicia.

OPPOSITE TOP:
BRÚ NA BÓINNE, NEWGRANGE
In the Newgrange part of the Brú na Bóinne complex are stones covered in megalithic art. Ireland has the largest concentration of megalithic art in Europe, particularly in the Boyne Valley, all of it abstract.

OPPOSITE LOWER:
KNOWTH MEGALITHIC PASSAGE TOMB
In the Brú na Bóinne complex is the Knowth passage tomb, which contains dozens of decorated stones, many with lunar and solar images. The world's oldest illustration of the moon is found at Knowth.

With the Romans invading Great Britain – and then ruling over most of it – Ireland came into the direct orbit of a literate culture. Roman and Greek texts started to mention Ireland. It was first called Hibernia by Julius Caesar.

However, there was little contact between Ireland and the Romans – ironic considering that Ireland was to become so important to Rome when the Vatican became the home of the Catholic Church. Ireland was never invaded by them, although there was trade between Ireland and Roman Britain – and raids conducted from the east coast of Ireland on Britain.

EARLY PREJUDICE

Earlier texts had referred to Ireland, and the derogatory opinions of the territory and its people were to be reflected through the centuries in watered-down versions by those who sought to subjugate Ireland. Diodorus Siculus, a Greek historian from Sicily, wrote in the first century BCE that Ireland's inhabitants ate human flesh. Strabo, a Roman Empire writer from what is now Turkey, wrote around the time of the birth of Christ that it had been reported the Irish considered it honourable to eat their dead fathers and openly have sex with their

OPPOSITE:
CALDRAGH GRAVEYARD, BOA ISLAND
Some of the first anthropomorphic stone figures in Ireland are found on Boa Island in Lough Erne, County Fermanagh. They stand in the Caldragh graveyard and are believed to represent Celtic deities.

BELOW:
GALLAGH MAN
Gallagh Man is the name given to a preserved body from 470–120 BCE found by peat-diggers at Gallagh, County Galway, in 1821. Examinations of the body found that the man had been about 1.8 metre (6ft) tall and 25 years old.

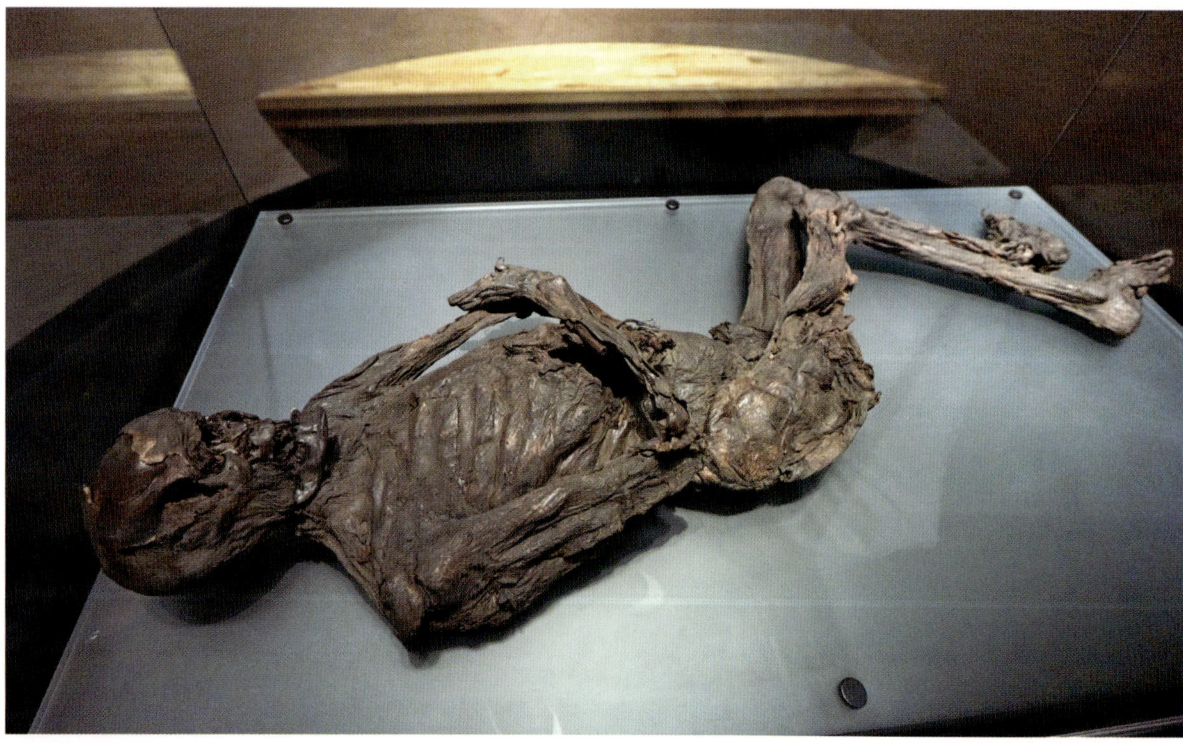

mothers and sisters. The Roman Pomponius Mela wrote in the first century that Ireland was unfavourable for growing grain but that it had so much grass, cattle would burst if they ate it unrestrained.

'LITTLE BRITAIN'

The Roman writer Tacitus recorded that his father-in-law, Gnaeus Julius Agricola, considered conquering Ireland while he was governor of Britain. Tacitus also said that most

LEFT:
BALLYSHANNON SUN DISC
This item from Donegal would likely have been worn and is made from a thin sheet of beaten gold. It is housed in the Ashmolean Museum in Oxford, who claim that it was found in 1669 by men looking for a place described in an old Irish song where 'a man of gigantic stature' was buried with gold ornaments.

OPPOSITE TOP:
STAIG STONE FORT
On the Iveragh Peninsula in County Kerry, this fort was built from local sandstone, without using mortar, and dates to around 300 BCE. Inside the fort there were ten flights of steps and two tiers.

OPPOSITE LOWER:
HILL OF TARA
County Meath's Tara – considered the ancient capital of Ireland – consists of a network of earthworks and former monuments that includes the Mound of the Hostages, where the remains of hundreds of people have been found.

BELOW:
CRANNOG, CONNEMARA
Crannogs were prehistoric artificial islands that were used as dwellings, particularly in Ireland and Scotland. This recreated one is on the County Galway coast, and only accessible by its causeway or by boat.

of the harbours and approaches to Ireland were known through commerce. In the second century, the Alexandrian Greek writer Ptolemy referred to Ireland as 'Little Britain', and detailed the locations of six promontories, 15 river mouths, 10 settlements and nine islands, and listed 16 population groups.

Although there is no evidence that the Romans invaded Ireland, there is still much speculation that they set foot on Irish soil, possibly in the form of an exploratory force. The second-century Roman author Juvenal wrote that Roman 'arms had been taken beyond the shores of Ireland'.

Tacitus wrote that an exiled Irish prince was in Roman-occupied Britain during the governorship of Agricola there, and he would later go back to Ireland to seize power. This story chimes with the Irish legend of Tuathal Techtmar. The son of a deposed Irish king, Techtmar is said to have taken back the family's crown in the first century after raiding his homeland from afar.

RAIDERS IN SCOTLAND

Rather than being invaded, the Irish were more used to carrying out invasions during this time, changing the course of history of Scotland in particular. People from Ireland who the Romans called the Scoti raided and settled in northern Britain in 367 CE – acts that would ultimately give Scotland its name. One set of these people who made Scotland their home was the Dal Riata, who, at the height of their power in the sixth and seventh centuries, had control over northeastern Ireland and much of the west coast of Scotland. The kingdom contained Argyll, which translates as 'coast of the Gaels'.

In these early centuries, the Irish also carried out raids in Cornwall, Wales and northwest England, with some settling in these areas. Even then, the Irish were emigrating, as they would continue to do for centuries, shaping the world so much.

SAINT PATRICK

It was the return route back across the Irish Sea that was to bring Christianity to Ireland, an event that was to colour the future of the Emerald Isle. Of course, Saint Patrick is credited with bringing the gospel to Ireland in 432, but some texts claim that there were already missionaries who had spread the word before his arrival.

And with Saint Patrick making the journey from Britain to Ireland – and with some Irish crossing in the other direction – so began a relationship between Britain and Ireland that was to have many a twist and turn over the coming centuries.

OPPOSITE:
CORLEA TRACKWAY
This roadway of oak planks in a boggy area of County Longford dates to the second century BCE. Experts – who are not completely certain of its purpose – say that it would have lasted only for a decade before sinking.

OVERLEAF:
DUNSEVERICK CASTLE, CO. ANTRIM
County Antrim is home to this castle, where it sits near the Giant's Causeway. Like that spectacular natural phenomenon, it is constructed from volcanic basalt, and Saint Patrick is recorded as having visited it in the fifth century.

THE COMING OF THE GOSPEL

Although Saint Patrick is credited with bringing Christianity to Ireland in the fifth century, little is known about him with certainty. But the fruits of the Christian revolution in Ireland laid at his feet are plentiful, not least in the many monasteries that sprang up around Ireland from the sixth century. They would go on to shape Irish society and become a binding force between sacred and secular Ireland.

A number of these monasteries were on the rocky peninsulas and islands of the southwest, where stone for building was easy to come by and the isolated locations offered monks the solitude they wanted for connecting with God. One of the most striking examples is Skellig Michael, an island off the Iveragh Peninsula in County Kerry, with its twin peaks overlooking a valley called Christ's Saddle. There still remain on the island domed stone huts used by the early monks.

ABBEYS AND MONASTERIES

Another notable sixth-century monastery was Clonard Abbey, next to the River Boyne in County Meath, founded by Saint Finnian. There he trained the 12 apostles of Ireland, who spread God's Word around the island and beyond. For Ireland was to become not just a land where Christianity could thrive, but also a place from which it could be adopted elsewhere.

Clonard became quite a development, and it is reported that it could accommodate 3000 students of Christianity. With the Roman Empire becoming extinct, such institutions also did much to maintain the study and writing of Latin.

Another monastery, Clonfert, in County Galway, was founded by Saint Brendan, who was one of the 12 apostles. Legend has it that he sailed west from Ireland and became the first European to set foot in America.

OPPOSITE:
SKELLIG MICHAEL MONASTERY
One of Ireland's early Christian monasteries was founded on this island off the coast of County Kerry and named after archangel Michael. The ruins were used to portray the home of Luke Skywalker in his later years in the *Star Wars* films.

SKELLIG MICHAEL
Skellig Michael was plundered in Viking raids in the ninth century, but the inhabitants – possibly only as many as 12 monks and an abbot – continued to live there for hundreds more years. It has more recently been a site for pilgrimage and tourism.

LEFT:
CLONFERT MONASTERY
Clonfert Cathedral in County Galway now stands where Saint Brendan founded a monastery and church in the sixth century. The cathedral dates from the 12th century and is in the Hiberno-Romanesque style.

OPPOSITE:
SAINT FINNIAN
At Saint Finnian's Roman Catholic church in the village of Clonard, County Meath, is a stained glass window showing the saint as a boy being taught in Wales by Saint David. Finnian would go on to found Clonard Abbey in the sixth century.

He is also said to have discovered an island that was called Saint Brendan's Island and lay somewhere west of Ireland in the Atlantic. But more reliable information than the manuscript written around 900 about his travels comes in the form of Atlantic wind patterns that, almost 600 years later, Christopher Columbus used to cross the ocean (by sailing west from the Canary Islands and taking a more northerly route back to western Europe).

SAINTS

Both Finnian and Brendan, who would become saints, were born in Ireland and baptized before devoting their life to Christ and spreading His word. As the fifth century became the sixth, through the seventh and into the eighth century, the practice of people being baptized – and some then joining the church – increasingly spread across Ireland.

Finnian and Brendan were at the forefront of this revolution, which swept across Ireland to such an extent that, as early as the sixth century, the Irish took Christianity back to Britain, Saint Patrick's birthplace.

In 563, another of the 12 apostles, Saint Columba, who was from Donegal, sailed to the Scottish island of Iona and set up a monastery there. By the time of his death in 597, Christianity was being preached right across northern and central Scotland, as well as on many of the islands. And in the seventh century, Irish monk Aidan was credited with converting Anglo-Saxons in Northumbria to Christianity. There he established Lindisfarne Priory. St Aidan's College at the University of Durham is named after him.

METAL WORKERS AND ART

In Ireland, Christianity had found a home where it could grow, be nurtured and act as a springboard for converting people in other parts of Europe. And it could shape a new culture in Ireland, too, partly thanks to Ireland's mineral and human resources. The island's people had a history of working with metals, whether native or imported, and they were used to expressing themselves visually with their rock art. Treasures such as the *Book of Kells*, the Ardagh Chalice and many carved stone crosses come from this period, between the arrival of Christianity and the Viking raids of the 800s.

SAINT BRENDAN THE NAVIGATOR

Hailing from southwest Ireland, Saint Brendan is honoured with a statue in the town of Bantry, County Cork. It was unveiled in 1968 to mark the opening of an oil terminal there, the outstretched arms of 'navigator' Brendan symbolically guiding the supertankers.

ABOVE:
SAINT PATRICK AND THE SNAKES
Saint Patrick is said to have driven the snakes out of Ireland, and he is celebrated worldwide as the land's patron saint.

OPPOSITE:
SAINT COLUMBA
From Donegal, Saint Columba is the patron saint of Derry, but is better known for having taken Christianity from Ireland to Scotland and popularised it there – but only after he had founded several monasteries in his homeland.

The *Book of Kells* is an illuminated manuscript, written in Latin and containing the four Gospels of the New Testament. It was created around 800, and is named for the Abbey of Kells, in County Meath, which was its home for centuries. It is considered a high point in the art emanating from Britain and Ireland in the early days of Christianity, with its 680 elaborately designed pages, using pigments imported from as far away as the Mediterranean. It is now kept in the library of Trinity College, Dublin.

The Ardagh Chalice is the chief feature of the Ardagh Hoard, which was found in 1868 by two boys digging in a potato field on the site of a former ringfort next to the village of Ardagh in County Limerick. The chalice is a large, two-handled beaten silver cup decorated with gold, gilt bronze, enamel, brass and lead pewter, and it was assembled from 354 separate pieces. The hoard also contained a copper-alloy cup and four brooches, and is now on display at the National Museum of Ireland in Dublin.

The stone crosses that were produced during this period were highly decorated and still dot the land.

OVERSEAS SCHOLARS

Just as Ireland was producing highly visible and prized objects to show its allegiance to God – and exporting the Christianity developing there to the likes of Scotland – it also started to attract Christian scholars from overseas to its monasteries.

In the eighth and ninth centuries, monasteries across western Europe flourished as the emperor Charlemagne – who ultimately controlled most of what is now France, Germany, the Low Countries, the Alpine countries and the northern half of Italy – decreed that every abbey should have a school.

COLUMBA

IONA ABBEY, SCOTLAND
Saint Columba founded a monastery on the Scottish island of Iona, from where he spread Christianity through the mainland. The illuminated Christian manuscript the *Book of Kells* was later produced by the monks of Iona.

As a result, there was much exchange in people and knowledge between the highly Christian Ireland and continental Europe.

SAINT COLUMBANUS

Saint Columbanus, who was born in Leinster in 543, founded a number of monasteries in the Frankish and Lombard kingdoms (modern-day Germany and northern Italy), such as Luxeuil Abbey in eastern France and Bobbio Abbey in Italy.

His influence also extended to northwestern France. Today in Saint-Malo in Brittany, there is a granite cross that carries his name. People would pray at it for rain in times of drought there, and the nearby village of Saint Coulomb commemorates him.

More recently, the Bishop of Hereford, John Oliver, suggested that Colombanus be the patron saint of motorcyclists, because he was so well travelled. The Vatican declared that he would be in 2002.

URBAN CENTRES

The spread of Christianity around Ireland led to certain locations gaining more importance – and drawing in people around them. Small towns started to form around some of the larger monasteries, such as Trim in County Meath and Lismore in County Waterford. Christianity was urbanizing Ireland, and Armagh was to become the ecclesiastical capital of Ireland, the seat of the Archbishops of Armagh and the Primates of All Ireland, for both the Roman Catholic Church and the Church of Ireland.

OPPOSITE:
SAINT AIDAN
Saint Aidan was from Ireland and schooled in the gospel on Iona before he founded a monastery on the island of Lindisfarne off the coast of Northumberland, where this statue of him stands. Early Christianity in northeast England had been largely displaced by Anglo-Saxon paganism before Aidan restored it.

Armagh has two cathedrals, which are both named after Saint Patrick, for it was he who started the chain of events that would lead to it having such religious significance.

PAGANS AND ST PATRICK

However, as with so much in Ireland, the paganism that was believed in for centuries before Christianity arrived is never far away. It was on the pagan ceremonial site of Navan Fort, on the western edge of Armagh, that Saint Patrick founded his church in 445.

According to the Leinster monk Muirchu, pagan chieftain Daire would not let Patrick build his church on the high land Patrick wanted, instead giving the Christian a low-lying area. When the chieftain's horses died while grazing on the church's land, he told his men to kill Patrick but then he himself fell ill. His men begged Patrick to save him, and Patrick gave him his holy water. Both Daire and his horses were revived, and in return Patrick was given a large bronze cauldron and the hill for his church.

POLYTHEISM TO CHRISTIANITY… AND WRITING

Although the pagan gods worshipped by the Celtic peoples of western Europe varied from region to region, there were some broad similarities. Toutatis was one, and he lives on today by being heavily evoked in the Asterix the Gaul comic books – about a tribe in Brittany holding out against Roman occupation. There is even a Toutatis rollercoaster at the Parc Asterix in France. Another Celtic god was Epona, a protector of horses, donkeys, ponies and mules, an indicator of the importance of livestock to these highly pastoral cultures.

With Christianity came belief in one god rather than the pagan polytheism that had been practised beforehand. And with it also came the written word; Ireland had previously had an oral culture. Ireland was to go on to have a highly literate population, and contribute some of the world's greatest writers.

And it all started with the spread of Christianity. Christianity also introduced formal organizational hierarchies to Ireland, started by Saint Patrick. He set up diocesan structures, with a hierarchy of bishops, priests and deacons.

CLAN RULE

But the monasteries did not develop in isolation from the clans that ruled secular Ireland. The two interacted. And – despite many monks, particularly in southwest Ireland, living in beehive-style stone huts called clochans, while the clans would hole themselves up in ringforts and promontory forts – lines were blurred between the two lifestyles. The monastic system began to adopt secular practices and forged ties with areas' ruling clans. Some members of monasteries married and had children, and some abbacies passed from father to son, rather than the monks remaining abstinent.

There were even skirmishes between monasteries, such as in County Offaly between the Clanmacnoise

OPPOSITE:
BOOK OF KELLS
The Christian illuminated manuscript the *Book of Kells* was created around 800 CE, after which treasures of Ireland's monasteries were dispersed because of Viking incursions.

BELOW:
TRINITY COLLEGE LIBRARY, DUBLIN
Since 1661, Trinity College Library has been home to the *Book of Kells*. It is also home to the 1916 Proclamation of the Irish Republic and the medieval harp used as the model for the Irish coat of arms and the Guinness trademark.

CHRISTI
SIMUS
NON

monastery and Durrow Abbey. In 764, 200 people were reported to have been killed in violence between the two. Meanwhile, high-born sons of Irish families started to join the church, with their families' approval. In 558 came the first of the high kings of Ireland, said to have been a Christian, Diarmait mac Cerbaill. And by 700, the church was fully part of Irish society.

CHANGING LANDSCAPE

However, in the second half of the eighth century, some institutions returned to asceticism, under the Rule of Saint Columbanus, which was stricter than the rules of Saint Benedict, who had been considered the founder of Western monasticism. Fasting was practised more, as was corporal punishment.

But monasteries amassed great wealth, and by the time of the first Viking invasion, the largest herds of livestock in Ireland were those owned by monasteries. By the ninth century, much of Ireland's forest had been cleared to make way for agriculture and grazing, to feed the expanding population, and the native Scots pine was cleared almost to extinction.

UÍ NÉILLS AND THE EÓGANACHTA

This period also saw a simplification of the make-up of the power dynamics in Irish secular society. The fifth to the eighth centuries saw Ireland change from being split roughly between five peoples (those in the Ulster, Connacht, Leinster, Munster and Meath areas) to those in two camps, the Uí Néills in the north and midlands and the Eoganachta in the south.

OPPOSITE TOP:
SAINT COLUMBANUS
This statue of Saint Columbanus is in Milan, showing how far his influence spread. Born in Leinster and educated at Bangor Abbey, he subsequently travelled throughout western Europe and founded a number of monasteries. He died in Bobbio, in northern Italy.

OPPOSITE LOWER:
ARDAGH CHALICE
The Ardagh Chalice is today housed in the National Museum of Ireland in Dublin. Of the two boys who found it in 1868 in County Limerick, Paddy Flanagan is buried in a local pauper's graveyard, and Jim Quin emigrated to Australia, and is buried in Melbourne. The chalice is valued at millions of dollars and even replicas sell for thousands.

BELOW:
ABBEY OF KELLS
The Abbey of Kells in County Meath was where the *Book of Kells* was kept for hundreds of years, until Oliver Cromwell's troops were stationed nearby. The abbey is said to have been founded by Saint Columba and built on an ancient hill fort.

ST MARY'S ABBEY
St Mary's Abbey in the Meath town of Trim was situated on the River Boyne and, until Henry VIII's dissolution of the monasteries, was a popular site for pilgrims believing in the healing powers of the abbey's statue of the Virgin Mary.

ST PATRICK'S CATHEDRAL, ARMAGH
This Catholic cathedral is the seat of the Primate of All Ireland. It was built between 1840 and 1904, replacing the medieval original, St Patrick's Cathedral, in the city, which was appropriated as an Anglican church during the Reformation.

ABOVE:
'THE BAPTISM OF THE KING OF CASHEL BY SAINT PATRICK'
This 18th century painting by James Barry shows the patron saint of Ireland baptising the king, who converted to Christianity in the fifth century.

LEFT:
ST PATRICK'S CHURCH OF IRELAND CATHEDRAL, ARMAGH
Saint Patrick himself is said to have founded a church on this site, and in the Middle Ages the cathedral's archbishop was the head of the Christian Church in Ireland. In the 11th century, the High King of Ireland Brian Boru was buried there.

The Ui Neills had the Hill of Tara and the significance of claiming to be king of all Ireland, but the Eoganachta also had a significant power base, emanating from the southwest. While this era may seem very male-dominated, with its male saints and clan leaders, one figure did emerge who was to become the 'mother saint' of Ireland.

SAINT BRIGID

Along with Patrick and Columba, the other national saint of Ireland was to be Brigid of Kildare. She founded the abbey in Kildare in the fifth century, as well as several convents. Since 2023, Saint Brigid's Day, 1 February, has been a public holiday in the Republic of Ireland. Again, there is a link to Ireland's pagan era – in pre-Christian times, the day was celebrated under the name Imbolc and marked the beginning of spring.

Ireland had entered the first years of the Common Era as pagan, but by the end of the eighth century it was Christian, and a significant power base for the church.

But all that was to come under threat from the Vikings, invaders who were very much in the pagan mould.

OPPOSITE:
SAINT BRIGID
Saint Brigid is the patroness saint of Ireland, and one of the three national saints, along with Patrick and Columba. She founded Kildare Abbey and many convents, and is the patroness of poetry and writing.

RIGHT:
ST BRIGID'S CATHEDRAL
Saint Brigid is said to have founded a church here in the fifth century, and a distinctive round bell tower was built alongside it.

BELOW:
BIDDY BOYS
Veneration of Saint Brigid has continued for centuries and a tradition has developed for 'Biddy Boys' to dress up and visit houses on Saint Brigid's Eve, 31 January. The tradition is most prevalent in southwest Ireland.

LEFT:
GRIANÁN OF AILEACH
This hillfort in Donegal was reconstructed in the 19th century, on a site that has been identified as the seat of the Kingdom of Aileach, one of the royal sites of Gaelic Ireland. The peak on which the fort stands overlooks the counties of Donegal, Londonderry and Tyrone.

OVERLEAF:
GUNDESTRUP CAULDRON
The Gundestrup Cauldron, found in a peat bog in Denmark, is typical of Celtic vessels used during the Iron Age in north-western Europe. Its ornate design denotes the importance that cauldrons had in these cultures at the time. A full-size replica stands in the National Museum of Ireland.

VIKINGS AND NORMANS

In 795, Vikings looted the island of Lambay, off the coast of eastern Ireland, just north of what is now the city of Dublin. Three years later they raided the Kingdom of Brega, on the eastern mainland. In 807, the west coast was affected, with a raid on Connacht. Thus began 200 years of raids from Scandinavia that unsettled an Ireland that was later seen to have been in the 'golden age' of Christian Irish culture. But the raids – particularly after Viking settlements started – also added to Ireland's culture, and its economy. From 821, Viking raids increased in frequency. The raiders were coming from the western fjords of Norway, travelling in longships and stopping off in the Shetlands, Orkneys and Scotland on their way. And they would soon be stopping off – on a not-so-temporary basis – in Ireland, too.

VIKING LONGPORTS

The Vikings established longports, where they could dock their boats and defend them and themselves against aggrieved communities. Here they would spend winter, rather than returning to Scandinavia.

The first longports were at Annagassan in County Louth, where the River Glyde meets the Irish Sea, and at Dublin. And from these bases, the Vikings would launch raids inland. In 837, it was reported that 60 longships were on the River Liffey, carrying 1500 men, and that another one of a similar size was sailing up the River Boyne.

From 837, the Vikings focused on sizeable targets, such as the larger monastic towns of Armagh, Glendalough, Kildare, Slane, Clonard, Clonmacnoise and Lismore.

OPPOSITE:
TRIM CASTLE
Trim Castle is one of Ireland's major landmarks dating from medieval times. As with so many of Ireland's pre-modern lasting relics, it stands near the River Boyne in County Meath. It was owned by the Wellesley family until the Duke of Wellington sold it. It was later used in the film *Braveheart*.

OLAF AND IVAR THE BONELESS

Two Norse leaders emerged from this time, Olaf and Ivar the Boneless, who effected a change in the power dynamics between the Irish and the Vikings. They formed an alliance with the king of Osraige, Cerball mac Dunlainge, against Mael Sechnaill. However, Cerball was later allied with Mael Sechnaill.

Olaf and Ivar had most of their success in the east and south of Ireland, developing ports there, at the expense of the north, where they met with much resistance from Aed Findliath.

IRISH VIKINGS

After Olaf and Ivar, Irish forces retook Dublin in 902. By now, the Vikings had worked their way into Irish society. For instance, a group of Vikings who were forced out of Ireland settled on the Wirral in northwest England, and with them were Irishmen. And St Bridget's Church in the Wirral's West Kirby is known to have been founded by 'Christian Vikings from Ireland'.

BELOW:
LANDINGS
An illustration showing Christian Irish opposing the landing of Danes at the River Liffey in the ninth century. The leader of the invading Vikings was Turgesius and Turgesius Island in Lough Lene, County Westmeath, takes his name.

OPPOSITE:
VIKING COIN
This Viking coin was minted in Ireland in the 11th century and is now housed in the British Museum in London. Since the Romans never conquered Ireland, coins first entered Ireland with the Vikings.

Although the Vikings took large swathes of England and France in their search for new territories and economic opportunities, however, they were unable to do so in Ireland because of the fractured nature of Irish society, with its clans. The Vikings couldn't just topple the ruling class of a large area and take the land, as they could in England and France, because in Ireland the various rulers had only small territories.

TRAVELLING SCHOLARS

Thanks to the Viking distraction, court scholars, who had become de rigueur in their strongholds, became less important to Irish kings. As a result, a number sought opportunities abroad. In the ninth century, the philosopher, poet and theologian John Scotus Eriugena was highly regarded for his works in what is now France and Germany.

LONGPORT AT LINN DÚACHAILL (ANNAGASSAN)
This is the site, on the River Glyde estuary in County Louth, where the Vikings' first 'longport' was established. Here, they could dock their ships and set up camp. In its time, Annagassan was as important to the Vikings' as the settlement further south that became Dublin.

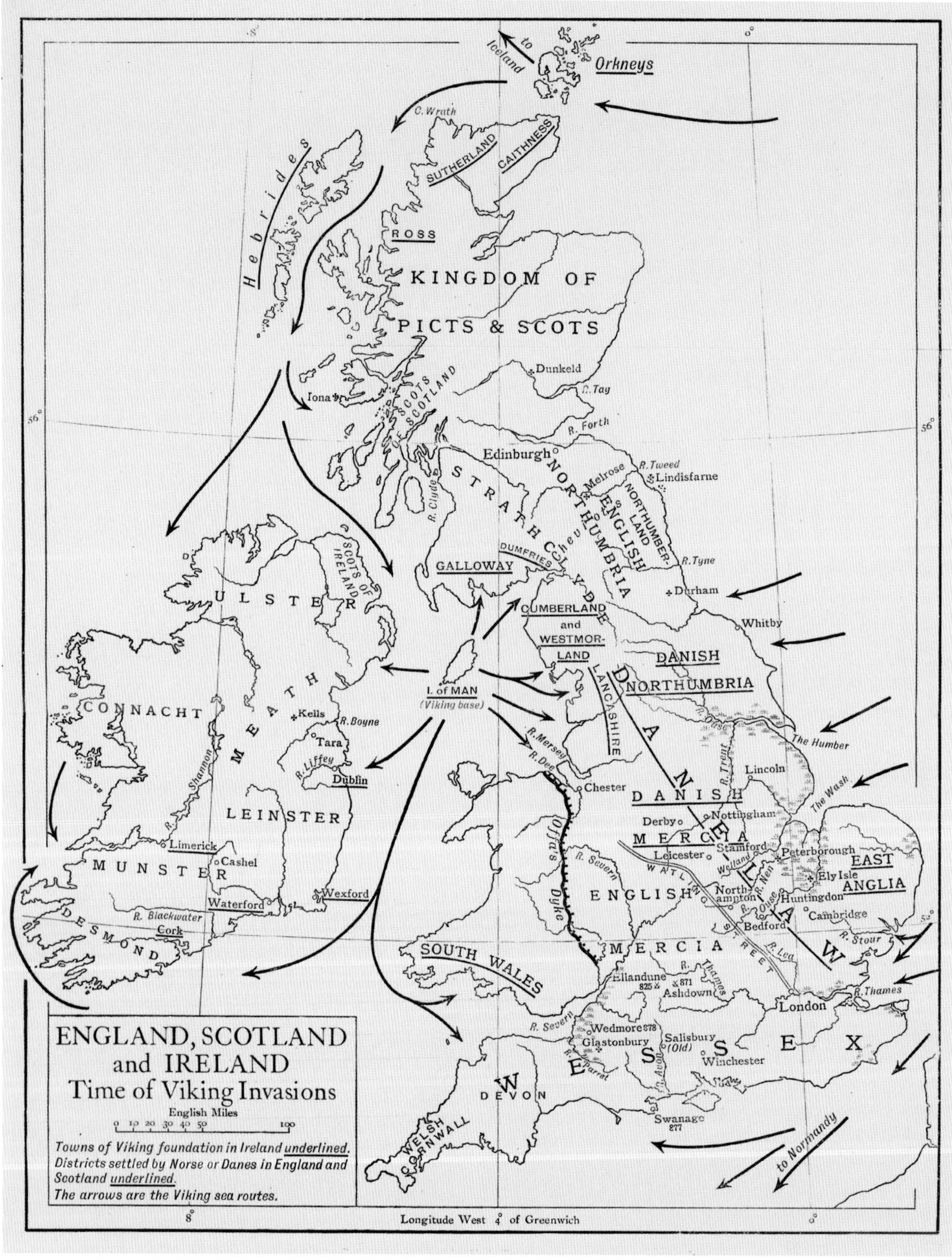
ENGLAND, SCOTLAND and IRELAND
Time of Viking Invasions
English Miles
Towns of Viking foundation in Ireland underlined.
Districts settled by Norse or Danes in England and Scotland underlined.
The arrows are the Viking sea routes.
to Iceland
Orkneys
C. Wrath
SUTHERLAND
CAITHNESS
Hebrides
ROSS
KINGDOM OF PICTS & SCOTS
Dunkeld
R. Tay
Iona
SCOTS OF SCOTLAND
R. Forth
Edinburgh
R. Tweed
Lindisfarne
Melrose
NORTHUMBRIA
ENGLISH
NORTHUMBERLAND
STRATHCLYDE
R. Clyde
Cheviots
DUMFRIES
GALLOWAY
R. Tyne
Durham
SCOTS OF IRELAND
ULSTER
CUMBERLAND and WESTMORLAND
Whitby
DANISH NORTHUMBRIA
LANCASHIRE
I. of MAN
(Viking base)
MEATH
CONNACHT
Kells
R. Boyne
Tara
R. Liffey
Dublin
R. Shannon
R. Mersey
R. Dee
Chester
R. Ouse
The Humber
R. Trent
Lincoln
The Wash
DANISH
DANELAW
Derby
Nottingham
MERCIA
Stamford
Leicester
Peterborough
EAST ANGLIA
Ely Isle
LEINSTER
Limerick
Cashel
MUNSTER
Offa's Dyke
R. Severn
WATLING STREET
R. Welland
R. Nen
North-ampton
Huntingdon
Cambridge
R. Ouse
Bedford
R. Stour
R. Lea
ENGLISH
MERCIA
Waterford
Wexford
R. Blackwater
Cork
DESMOND
SOUTH WALES
Ellandune 825
871 Ashdown
R. Thames
London
Wedmore 878
Glastonbury
Salisbury (Old)
Winchester
R. Avon
R. Parret
WESSEX
DEVON
WELSH CORNWALL
Swanage 877
to Normandy
Longitude West 4° of Greenwich

And Sedulius Scottus became the foremost writer among a group of Irish scholars in Liege, in what is now Belgium. The Irish would have strong links on the continent for centuries, and part of that was down to the Vikings driving away some of the most valued.

In 914 a new Viking fleet appeared in Waterford Harbour, and Norsemen landed in Leinster too. Dublin fell again to the Vikings, who enlarged the settlement, as they did in Waterford, Cork, Wexford and Limerick. They also founded new coastal towns and settled there, with a group of people with mixed Norse and Irish heritage developing.

OPPOSITE:
MAP OF BRITISH ISLES, 9TH–11TH CENTURIES
This map of the British Isles shows the Viking incursions from the east. The Vikings that specifically populated Ireland came from the north, having previously made landings in Scotland and its islands. For the Vikings, the Isle of Man was a focal point for the British Isles.

FIRST KING OF IRELAND

It wasn't until the emergence of Brian Boru in Munster in the late tenth century that the Vikings were seriously threatened by the Irish. He defeated the Norse of Limerick in 977 and 20 years later he was

BELOW:
ANNAGASSAN HARBOUR
The area that the Vikings picked for their first longport later became a place where fishing vessels would moor, and a village developed on the coast. The Viking heritage of the area is still marked and the locality is known for Viking-themed festivities.

5A
6A
7A
8A

OSEBERG SHIP
The Oseberg ship is one of the finest examples in existence of a Viking longboat. It was found in a burial mound in Norway and is believed to date from the eighth or ninth century. It is now on display with some of its contents in Oslo.

acknowledged as the ruler of southern Ireland. By 1011 every major regional king had submitted to him, so he is now seen as the first real king of Ireland.

NORSE IMPRINT

The Vikings had never had complete dominion over the whole of Ireland, but they had left a huge imprint, and there were now flourishing towns across the land, and increased trading opportunities, such as with the Kingdom of the Isles, the Norse-Gaelic kingdom comprising the Isle of Man, the Hebrides and the islands of the Clyde.

After Brian Boru, Ireland was more unified and economically prosperous, and this period saw the building of its first castles.

ABOVE:
BRIAN BORU
Eleventh century High King of Ireland Brian Boru is credited with bringing to an end the Viking invasions. Having made himself King of Munster, he moved east and took Leinster to become the High King. He founded the O'Brien dynasty.

BELOW:
CELTIC ROUND TOWER
This fine example of a Celtic round tower stands at Clonmacnoise in County Offaly. As well as being used as bell towers, the structures were useful at monasteries for defensive and lookout purposes.

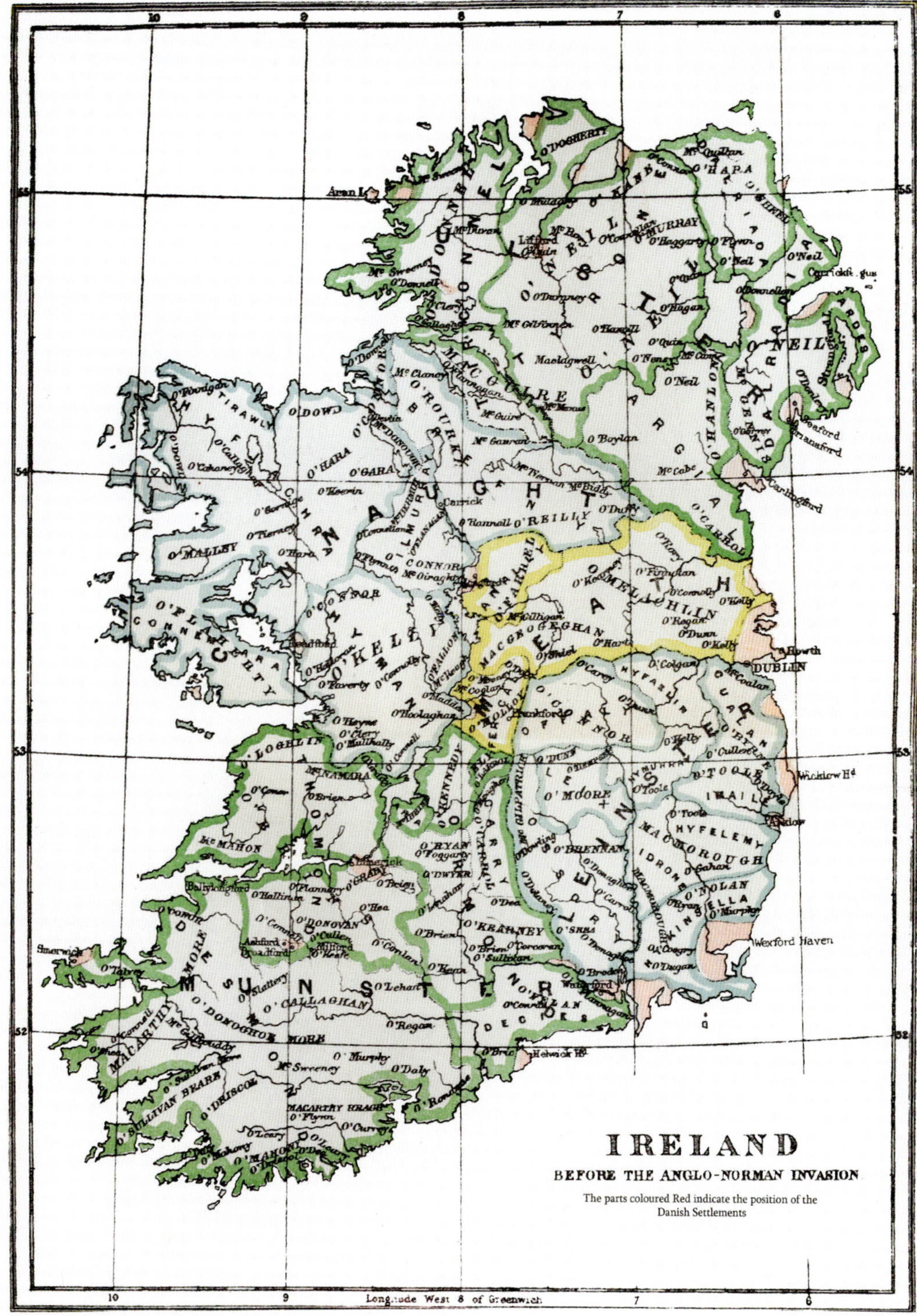

MEDIEVAL IRELAND – PROVINCES
This map shows how Ireland was divided into provinces just before the Normans invaded. The areas shaded red – mostly coastal areas, particularly in the southeast – mark where the Vikings had settled.

BATTLE OF CLONTARF (1014)
Hugh Frazer's 1826 painting of the Battle of Clontarf, which took place in 1014 near Dublin. The forces of High King of Ireland Brian Boru routed an alliance of Viking and other Irish forces. Boru was killed in the battle.

NORMAN INCURSIONS

In neighbouring England, by the twelfth century Norman control was well established, following the famous invasion of 1066, and the Normans were soon to come to Ireland's shores.

Diarmait Mac Murchada, a deposed king of Leinster, sought permission from Henry II of England to recruit Norman knights to help regain his kingdom. They arrived in 1167, followed by further forces. Diarmait named his son-in-law, the Norman Richard de Clare, as his heir.

ENGLISH INTEREST

Fearing a rival Norman state in Ireland, Henry ordered large forces to land in Ireland, which they did at Waterford in 1171. Henry awarded Irish territories to his son John who, when he became king of England, also claimed the 'lordship of Ireland'.

The Normans controlled Ireland's east coast but suffered rebellion at the hands of Fineen MacCarthy in the thirteenth century, and the Irish won back large tracts of land. They also came under attack from Edward Bruce of Scotland, who launched an invasion, but was defeated.

OPPOSITE:
SIEGE AT WATERFORD (1170)
This illustration shows resistance to Henry II's Norman army in Waterford. As well as Waterford, the forces would claim Dublin, under Earl of Pembroke, Richard 'Strongbow' de Clare.

BELOW:
HENRY II AT WATERFORD
When Henry II landed in Ireland in 1171, he was the first English king to do so, and his visit would be the start of 800 years of English domination. Henry II's invasion had the blessing of the Roman Catholic Church, which wanted to re-assert its influence over Ireland.

VISITOR RECEPTION
FÁILTIÚ
STATE APARTMENTS
NA SEOMRAÍ STÁIT
CONFERENCE CENTRE

DUBLIN CASTLE
The Record Tower of Dublin Castle was built in the 13th century, the castle having been commissioned by King John of England. The castle's job was defence of the growing city of Dublin, the administration of justice and the protection of the King's treasures.

IRELAND
IN THE MIDDLE AGES
Showing
PRINCIPAL FAMILIES AND CLANS
Scale of Miles
0 10 20 30 40 50
10° 9° 8° 7° 6°
55° 54° 53° 52°
North Channel
O'Doherty
TYRCONNELL
O'Donnell
Foyle
DE BURGH
Bann
Carrickfergus
O'Flynn
ULSTER
TYRONE
O'Neill
L. Neagh
L. Erne
Mc Guire
Blackwater
O'Hanlon
Magennis
Downpatrick
LAWLESS
Sligo
O'Dowd
BREFFNY
O'Rorke
McMahon
URIEL
Dundalk
L. Conn
Achill I.
O'Malley
O'Reilly
CONNAUGHT
DE BURGH
(BURKE)
L. Mask
Roscommon
O'Connor
ANGHAILE
NUGENT
Kells
MORTIMER
Trim
Boyne
PLUNKET
THE ENGLISH PALE
Drogheda
MEATH
DE LACY
L. Ree
O'Flaherty
L. Corrib
O'Kelly
Athlone
Dublin
Liffey
Galway
Molloy
OFFALY
O'Connor
FITZGERALD
O'Shaughnessy
Shannon
O'Byrne
O'Toole
Aran Is.
L. Derg
Roscrea
LEIX
MORTIMER
Carlow
Wicklow
O'Brien
THOMOND
CLARE
LEINSTER
BUTLER
Arklow
BUTLER
O'More
BIGOD
Kilkenny
OSSORY
CLARE
Nore
Barrow
Slaney
Limerick
R. Shannon
FITZGERALD
FITZGIBBON
Suir
McMurrough
VALENCE
FITZMAURICE
MUNSTER
BUTLER
Clonmel
Wexford
Tralee
Waterford
Blackwater
FITZGERALD
O'Sullivan
DESMOND
Cork
Lee
Mc Carthy
Bandon
Kinsale
O'Donovan
Norman Families thus .... CLARE
Irish Clans .... O'Kelly
Boundary of the Pale in the XV Century
Castles ◇ Boroughs ○
GOLDSCHMIDT & HAMPEL N.Y.
9° West from Greenwich 8°

ABOVE:
HENRY VIII AND FAMILY
The story of Ireland was to irrevocably change with the Tudor conquest of the land on the orders of English King Henry VIII. The Anglo-Norman invasion had conquered parts of Ireland, but rebellion from Irish chiefs and the Black Death was to force the English to scale back their ambitions. The reign of Henry VIII and his descendants was to introduce Protestantism to Ireland and claim the whole island for the English.

OPPOSITE:
THE 'ENGLISH' PALE
This map shows the 'Pale' – the area of Ireland governed by the English – in the late Middle Ages, and the names of the chief Irish and Norman families living in Ireland then. The Pale extended from south of Dublin north to Dundalk. The word – which has entered general usage with the term 'beyond the pale' – was also used to refer to the area controlled by the English at Calais.

The Normans' attempt to take Ireland was also impeded by disease. When the Black Death arrived in 1348, the worst-hit areas were where people lived closely together, such as towns and villages, and this affected Norman areas more than the more dispersed, agricultural Irish ones.

BEYOND THE PALE

The Norman-controlled area shrank to an area around Dublin called the Pale, hence the English expression for something unsavoury being 'beyond the pale'. Meanwhile, the Norman lords who lived 'beyond the Pale' had, by the fifteenth century, adopted Gaelic culture – so much so, that these Hiberno-Norman families were said to be 'more Irish than the Irish'.

With the Hundred Years War, and then the Wars of the Roses, distracting the English, Ireland fell down the list of priorities. However, with the coming to the throne of Henry VIII, Ireland was to become the focus of new religious division that was to dominate its fortunes for the next half a millennium.

PROTESTANTS AND CATHOLICS

Before Henry VIII, religion was not an issue in Ireland – both the Irish and the invading English were Catholic. But with Henry's split from Rome, he wanted all his lands to fall under his church. However, Ireland, with its different history from England's, did not readily comply, and so a series of measures were put in place to make Catholics second-class citizens in Ireland – measures that ran throughout the 16th, 17th, 18th and 19th centuries.

At the same time English – and increasingly Scottish – Protestants were imported, particularly in the north, as the ruling class and as owners of land taken from dispossessed Catholics. And so Ireland became divided on religious grounds, as it still is today.

IRISH REBELLION

In 1509, when he inherited the English crown, Henry VIII also became lord of Ireland, as had all of the kings of England since the Anglo-Norman invasion in the twelfth century. In 1534, when the ninth earl of Kildare, the lord deputy of Ireland, died in the Tower of London, accused of corruption and maladministration, his son, known as 'Silken Thomas', began a rebellion in Dublin. Previously, the Kildare dynasty had invited Burgundian troops into Dublin to crown the Yorkist pretender Lambert Simnel as king of England in 1487.

Thomas – whose nickname came about because he and his troops wore silk fringes on their helmets – publicly renounced his

OPPOSITE:
JERPOINT ABBEY
Jerpoint Abbey is a ruined monastery in County Kilkenny that was founded in the 12th century. Its fate was sealed with Henry VIII's dissolution of the monasteries, in which he ordered all such establishments under his control to be closed.

OVERLEAF:
MERCENARIES
Albrecht Dürer's 1521 drawing of Irish mercenaries shows soldiers that he encountered in Europe. From its earliest days, Ireland had links to Europe and there had been exchange in goods and people between Ireland and the continent for centuries.

allegiance to his cousin, Henry VIII, at St Mary's Abbey in Dublin. His forces attacked Dublin Castle but were routed by the king's and he was executed in 1537.

ABOVE:
THE EARL OF KILDARE RENOUNCING HIS ALLEGIANCE TO HENRY VIII
This 1854 drawing shows Thomas Fitzgerald renouncing his cousin Henry VIII's rule in 1534. This event – at Saint Mary's Abbey, Dublin – would spark a rebellion against the king. Dublin Castle held out against the rebellion and it was put down.

OPPOSITE:
LAMBERT SIMNEL BEING PRESENTED TO THE EARL OF KILDARE
This scene shows Lambert Simnel, pretender to the English throne, being presented to the Earl of Kildare in 1487. Kildare, the head of the Irish government, embraced him, challenging Henry VII's rule. Kildare's grandson would subsequently lead the rebellion against Henry VIII.

KINGDOM OF IRELAND

As a response, Henry VIII created the Kingdom of Ireland in 1542 as a dependency of England, with him as king. He sought to quell any further uprisings through a system of 'surrender and regrant', developed with the help of Thomas Cromwell. Under this, clan chiefs would be brought under English law, and would be granted English titles and seats in the parliament in Dublin. England was already undergoing its Reformation – in 1534, Henry VIII had confirmed his supremacy over the church in England, after the Pope refused to annul his marriage to Catherine of Aragon. And English attempts to undermine the Catholic Church were unleashed in Ireland as well as England, but faced much greater resistance in Ireland, with effects that would transform the country.

Henry VIII installed his own archbishop of Dublin and decreed that Catholics loyal to the Holy See were to be prosecuted as traitors. A year later, he introduced legislation in the Irish parliament regarding closure of the monasteries. However, only 16 out of the 400 religious houses in Ireland were closed.

Determined, Henry continued to press for the monasteries' closure and, under the 'surrender and regrant' scheme, local lords were promised the riches of the monasteries if they swore allegiance to the new Irish crown.

STONE CARVINGS OF MONKS AT JERPOINT ABBEY

Monks carved in stone at Jerpoint Abbey, which became notable for its religious imagery. It was also a site of pilgrimage to the grave of its Cistercian founder Bishop Felix O'Dullany. Local legend has it that the grave of Saint Nicholas lies close to Jerpoint Abbey. The monks of the abbey are said to have survived the dissolution of the monasteries, only to be killed later by Oliver Cromwell's forces.

ASSAULT ON THE MONASTERIES

But by the time Henry died in 1547, only half of Ireland's monasteries had closed, and the houses of friars continued to thrive.

Although the introduction of Protestantism to the British Isles as the state religion was Henry VIII's doing, it was Henry's son and successor Edward VI who formally secured it. However, on his death, there was then an about-turn for five years, after the Catholic Queen Mary came to the throne.

When Mary died in 1558 and Elizabeth I was crowned, Henry VIII's plans for the spread of his church throughout the British Isles would now have almost half a century – under the long reign of the Protestant Queen Elizabeth – to be realized. Under Elizabeth, attendance at the new, Protestant Church of Ireland services became obligatory across the island, with fines and physical punishments as penalties for those who refused.

PLANTATIONS

Elizabeth I also pressed ahead with the Irish plantations plan, which had been started under Mary. settlers were given land to farm, to bring Ireland more into the English fold; to effect this, some lands were taken from the Irish. To begin with, this was not an overt attempt to fill Ireland with Protestants at the expense of Catholics, but its outcome was that areas where there were a greater number of plantations had a greater number of Protestants, which would go on to cause previously unseen division along religious lines across Ireland.

In fact, under Mary, the Plantation of Queen's County (named after Catholic Mary) and King's County (after Catholic King Philip of Spain) were established in the counties that are now Offaly and Laois. And county towns called Philipstown (now Daingean) and Maryborough (Portloaise) were created.

REBELLION

The resident Irish did not stand idly by. In the 1550s the O'Moore and O'Connell clans rebelled over being displaced for the plantations. And in 1569, the Earl of Desmond in Munster rebelled against the extension of English state power over Ireland – and the enforcement of Protestantism – by having his forces attack the English colony of Kerrycurihy, near

LEFT:
DISSOLUTION OF THE MONASTERIES
Henry VIII's dissolution of the monasteries, between 1536 and 1541, was completed under the Act of Supremacy that made Henry VIII the absolute head of the Church of England, the country separating from Rome. With this, Anglicanism became the official religion of England and Ireland, leading to persecution of those who refused to convert.

THOMAS CROMWELL

Thomas Cromwell was Henry VIII's first minister and a prime figure in the reformation. He engineered the annulment of the marriage between the king and Catherine of Aragon, so Henry could marry Anne Boleyn, after Pope Clement VII had barred it. This led to Henry becoming supreme head of the Church of England. Henry later accused Cromwell of treason and he was executed.

ON SINE SOLE
IRIS.

Cork, and then Cork itself and Kilkenny. But the rebellion was put down, with its military leader, James FitzMaurice, exiled.

COUNTER-REFORMATION WARS

Ten years later, FitzMaurice landed in Munster from Europe with Spanish and Italian troops, having declared himself a soldier of the Counter-Reformation. With backing from the Pope, he joined up with other lords, including a Desmond, but retribution from the English was severe, with the Desmond lands ransacked and FitzMaurice killed. Further uprisings were also put down with force – so much so that the lord deputy of Ireland, Lord Grey de Wilton, was recalled by Elizabeth I for excessive brutality.

OPPOSITE:
ELIZABETH I
Under Elizabeth I's rule, rebellions by the Irish against English rule were put down mercilessly. She also handed out Irish land to courtiers to prevent Spain from having bases from which to attack England.

BELOW:
THE MURDER OF THE EARL OF DESMOND
Gerald Fitzgerald, Earl of Desmond, was murdered in 1583, which put an end to a revolt in Munster that he had engineered with Spanish and Italian help.

OVERLEAF:
SIEGE OF KINSALE
Four thousand Spaniards landed near Kinsale, County Cork, in 1601 to support the Irish in a rebellion against the English rulers. The English forces ended the revolt and in 1603 a peace treaty was signed with Spain.

Morass
Milord Deputeits läger
rlandt welchs vbr die dreissig Iahr
Sich endtlich noch bezwingen lest,
Vnd eusser

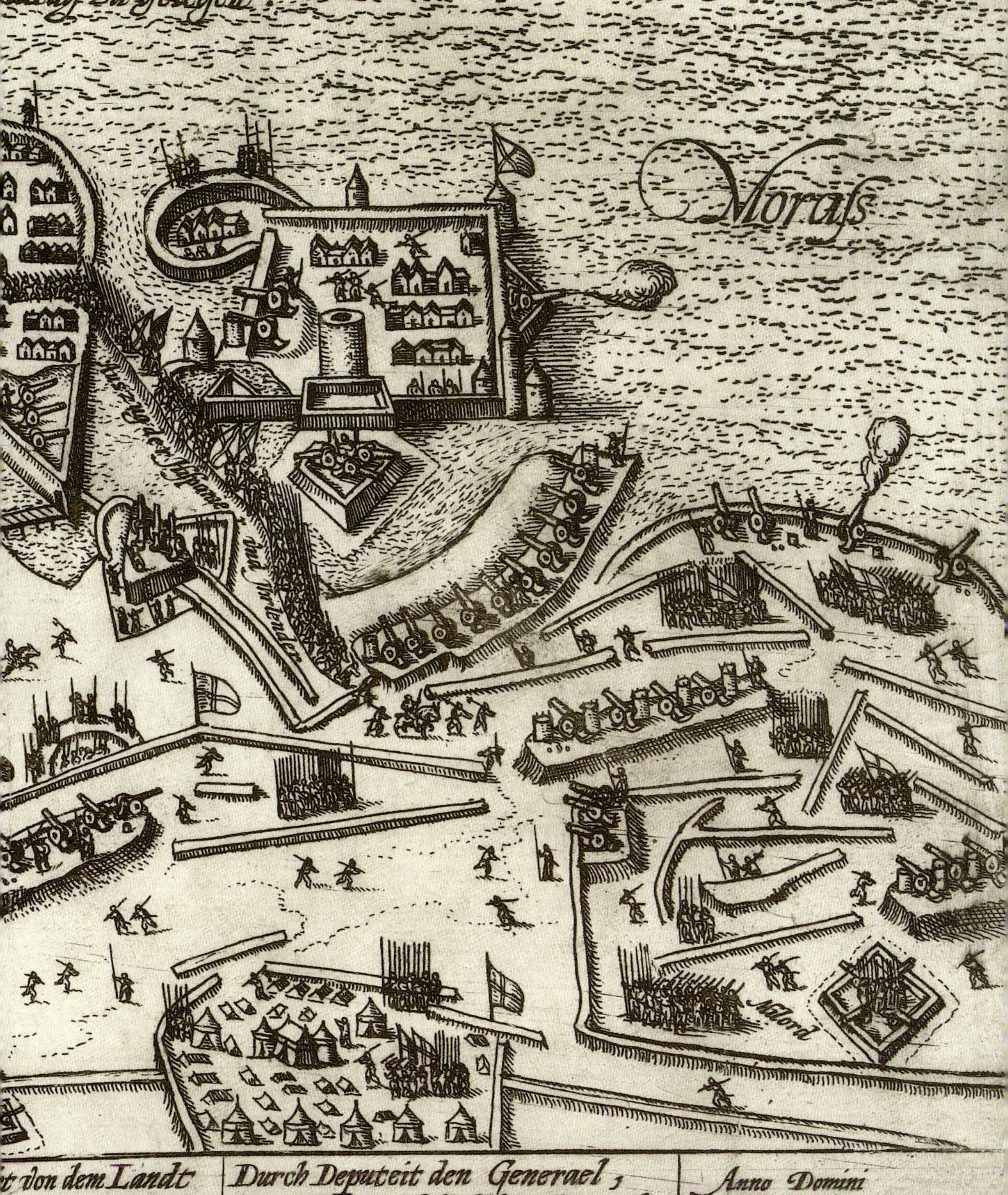
tat vnd Ves tung
YNSAEL
men, im mitten des Seestrandes
Mittag zu gelegen
Morass
t von dem Landt
Konigin handt .
Durch Deputeit den Generael ,
Der Tyrons volck schlug allzumael .
Anno Domini
1602 . 8 . Janar.

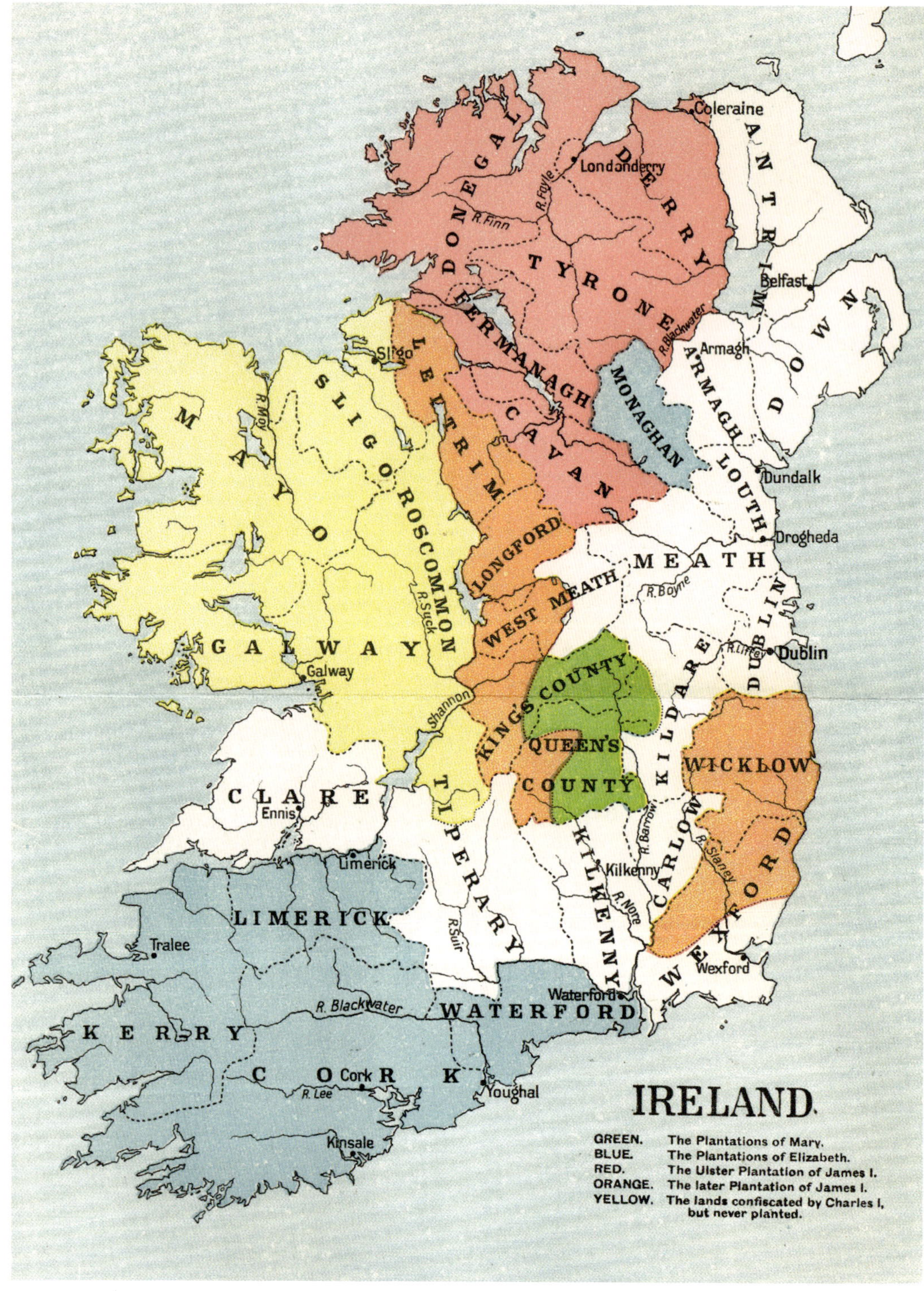

ABOVE:
PLANTATION OF IRELAND
Successive English kings and queens from Mary onwards carved up Ireland for their Plantations, confiscating Irish-owned land and distributing to settlers from Great Britain, with Mary's settlement of Ulster being the most successful.

OPPOSITE:
SIR WALTER RALEIGH
In 1579 and 1580, Walter Raleigh took part in the quelling of Irish rebellions. For this, the adventurer was rewarded with land in Munster. He became the mayor of Youghal, where his house still stands.

ÆTATIS
AN
MOR ET VIRTUTE

LEFT:
HUGH O'NEILL, EARL OF TYRONE
This earl, from the O'Neill clan, raised an army to battle Elizabethan rule, despite spending his early life being seen as a potential 'puppet ruler' by the English. His rebellion ended with the Siege of Kinsale, after which he fled to Rome, where he died.

After three years of war, Munster suffered a severe famine, and there was an outbreak of plague in Cork, to which people had fled to escape the fighting. In April 1582, the provost marshal of Munster, Sir Warham St Leger, estimated that 30,000 people had died of hunger in the previous six months.

The thousands of imported English soldiers and administrators who participated in the suppressing of the rebellions were rewarded with territory in the Munster Plantation, made up of lands confiscated from the Desmonds. English explorer Sir Walter Raleigh was the recipient of the largest grant of lands in Munster.

Later in the sixteenth century came the Nine Years War, which was started in the north of Ireland by Hugh O'Neill and Hugh Roe O'Connell, who were rebelling against English rule. The rebellion spread across the whole of Ireland, and had backing from Catholic Spain, but was effectively ended by the English with the Siege of Kinsale. In 1607, the Irish rebels and their families and followers departed for Europe (known as the flight of the earls), which marked a turning point in Anglo–Irish relations, with the English having the upper hand and able to pursue their plantation policy, in particular earmarking the lands vacated by the earls for the new Plantation of Ulster.

INCREASING DIVISIONS

The plantation policy expanded to Sligo, Fermanagh and Monaghan, and wholescale immigration from Protestant England – and increasingly Scotland – fostered anti-Protestant sentiment within the Irish population, which was spurred by Pope Pius V declaring Elizabeth I a heretic in 1570. And it was not just the Gaelic Irish who felt treated as second-class citizens by the English; so did those descended from Anglo-Norman settlers – termed the 'Old English' – who reaffirmed their commitment to Rome.

The international links that the Irish had forged during the Viking invasions also came to bear fruit – many of the Catholic clergy supporting the Counter-Reformation had been educated in seminaries on the continent, and Irish colleges had been established in many countries in Catholic Europe for the training of Irish Catholic priests and the education of Irish Catholic gentry.

ABOVE:

RALEIGH'S ESTATE MAP

This map, from 1598, is the oldest estate map in Ireland. It shows Walter Raleigh's land at Mogeely in County Cork. Although Raleigh popularised the potato in England and Ireland, having brought them back from his travels to America, it is more likely that they had were originally introduced into Ireland by Spanish traders.

NEW PROTESTANT COMMUNITY

But by the end of the Tudor conquest of Ireland, in the early 17th century, English law ruled over the land, and there was now a sizeable Protestant community in charge, subjugating an aggrieved Catholic majority. By 1641, the largest of the plantations, Ulster, had settled up to 80,000 English and Scots, with many of the new 'Ulster Scots' predominantly Presbyterian. This area had once been the most Gaelic Irish part of Ireland – upon which England had little influence – but the flight of the earls and the Plantation of Ulster had turned the north of Ireland into the part of the island over which England had most control.

STRENGTHENING ENGLISH POWER

The Scottish influence over Ulster was partly as a result of the accession of James VI of Scotland to the English throne as James I of England. He saw the Plantation of Ulster as a joint 'British' venture. To lessen the likelihood of rebellion – as in Munster

FLIGHT OF THE EARLS

On 14 September 1607, rebel Hugh O'Neill – together with his co-conspirator Hugh O'Donnell, 1st Earl of Tyrconnell – left Ireland with their families, household staff, followers and other nobility. In total about 90 people fled, ending up in Rome. In 2007, on the 400th anniversary of the flight, a sculpture was unveiled commemorating the event, in the coastal village of Rathmullan in Donegal, from where the earls had departed.

LEFT:
MASSACRES
This illustration shows Protestant settlers being massacred by local Catholics on Portadown Bridge, County Armagh, over the River Bann. The incident happened in November 1641, and Protestants were either stabbed to death, shot or forced into the river. This and other massacres were used to justify the Cromwellian invasion of Ireland.

OPPOSITE:
OLIVER CROMWELL
In 1649, Oliver Cromwell completed his overthrow of Charles I by having him executed, and Irish Catholics signed an alliance with English royalists. Cromwell subsequently invaded Ireland. Before his invasion, Parliamentarian forces held outposts only in Dublin and Derry. By the time Cromwell departed, in 1650, they were in control of most of eastern and northern Ireland, having gained strongholds such as Drogheda and Wexford.

– the new landowners were banned from taking on Irish tenants. So they imported farmers from England and Scotland. And the so-called 'planters' were forbidden from selling their lands to any Irishman, further disenfranchising the host population.

PERSECUTION AND UPRISING

Catholics were barred from public office and serving in the army, and the lands of the Roman Catholic Church were handed to the Protestant Church of Ireland.

In 1641, Irish Catholics, led by Felim O'Neill, rebelled against Protestant domination, a movement that spread across the classes and was supported by most Irish Catholic lords. In this uprising there were a number of massacres of Protestant settlers in Ulster.

ENGLISH CIVIL WAR

With civil war breaking out in England in 1642 – after King Charles I refused to consider the will of parliament – there were no English troops available to put down the uprising, and the rebels were left in control of most of Ireland. They ruled the country as Confederate Ireland from 1642 to 1649 and allied themselves with Charles I and the English royalists, because Charles was not a committed Protestant, and showed Catholic tendencies in his choice of wife and church services.

=The royalists were defeated by the parliamentarians, Charles I was executed and the parliamentarians chose Oliver Cromwell to reconquer Ireland, since the remaining English royalists had formed an alliance with Confederate Ireland.

OPPOSITE:
SIEGE OF DROGHEDA (1649)
To gain Drogheda, Cromwell's forces killed a number of civilians as well as Irish and royalist forces. The town had been the setting of a previous siege, in 1641, when the Irish had wrested control of it from English forces. At the time, those English were royalists, but the execution of Charles I and ascendancy of the Protestant parliament had made allies of the Irish and royalists.

RIGHT:
RICHARD TALBOT, EARL OF TYRCONNELL
Under the restoration of the monarchy in England, Irishman Richard Talbot helped to reclaim land for Catholics that had been taken from them under Cromwell. The earldom of Tyrconnell was recreated for him and he became first earl.

CROMWELL IN IRELAND

A fervent enemy of the Roman Catholic Church, Cromwell was ruthless in his approach to retaking Ireland. After landing in Dublin, his forces captured Wexford and Drogheda. At Drogheda, his troops killed nearly 3500 people after the town fell – about 2700 royalist soldiers, along with all the men in the town carrying arms, including some civilians, prisoners and Roman Catholic priests.

In the Act of Settlement 1652, Catholics were barred from towns and from marrying Protestants. However – after the failure of Oliver Cromwell's son Richard to continue his late father's legacy – with the Restoration of England's monarchy under Charles II and James II, Irish Catholics were allowed back into the Irish parliament and the army. Some also received compensation and land grants, which many Irish Protestants felt was unjust given the massacres of Protestant civilians by Catholics in 1641.

JACOBITE RESISTANCE

In 1688, fears among high-ranking English Protestants that James II was about to start a new Catholic dynasty with the birth of his son led to the king being deposed in favour of his Protestant daughter Mary and her Dutch husband William of Orange. Richard Talbot, a Catholic who had been appointed lord deputy of Ireland in the Restoration, raised an army of Irish Catholic supporters of James – Jacobites – and James, with the help of King Louis XIV of France, sailed to Ireland, seeking a safe haven.

A Williamite force landed at Carrickfergus and advanced to Dundalk and, in 1689, William himself landed with a force of British, Dutch and Danish troops. The following year, at the Battle of the Boyne, James's forces were defeated. James fled to France and, in 1691, the Jacobite resistance was ended at the Battle of Aughrim.

Penal laws on Catholic land ownership in Ireland were subsequently re-applied with vigour and, over the century following 1691, Catholic land ownership fell from 14 per cent to around five per cent.

BATTLE OF THE BOYNE (1690)

Following the Glorious Revolution of 1688, the Jacobites were swept away in favour of William of Orange and his wife Mary. Protestant England again tried to reassert its authority over Ireland, which culminated in the Battle of the Boyne, near Drogheda, in July 1690. The Williamite forces defeated James II's troops. The battles of the Boyne and Aughrim – both victories for the government – have been marked in recent years in Northern Ireland with summer Protestant marches, which Catholics have seen as provocative.

A LOST CAUSE
King James II left Ireland – never to return – after the Battle of the Boyne in 1690. He left from Duncannon, County Wexford, sailing to France. His son and then grandson (the 'old pretender' and the 'young pretender') both tried to reinstate a Jacobite on to the English throne, in 1715 and then in 1745, both without success.

ABOVE:
FLIGHT OF THE WILD GEESE
In 1691, at the Treaty of Limerick, the Irish cause was accepted as lost, but Jacobite soldiers were given the opportunity to flee overseas. Hence the so-called Flight of the Wild Geese, in which Jacobites set sail for France. Women and children tried to join them, but some perished in the sea.

OPPOSITE:
HENRY GRATTAN, MP
Born into a protestant Anglo-Irish family, Henry Grattan became a member of both the Dublin and London parliaments, where he campaigned in the late 18th and early 19th centuries for Ireland to govern itself while still being a Crown territory. Grattan Bridge in Dublin is named in his honour.

But Catholics were not the only group persecuted by the English. In 1704, Presbyterians were also barred from holding public office, as the English Anglican elite distrusted the Scottish Presbyterian community, which had become the majority in Ulster.And so began a long period – branded 'the long peace' – in which those who followed the Anglican Church of Ireland ruled Ireland without interruption, at the expense of the Catholics and Presbyterians, the latter of whom also had virtually no political power. Although there was an Irish parliament in Dublin, its effect was small and Ireland was, in essence, run from London. England's draconian methods worked. Catholic landed gentry converted to Protestantism to keep their lands and, because the penal laws also worsened the economic outlook for Catholics by stipulating that their property could not be passed on to a single heir, estates were split up into increasingly small parcels until they were unviable and sold (to Protestants). Both Catholics and Presbyterians were also barred from jobs in the legal profession.

ANGLO-IRISH RULE

Many of those ruling Ireland did so in absentia, but, as in so many places in the world where those in the elite live in the country they are ruling for long periods, some grew attached to what had become their homeland. And so there developed a class of Anglo-Irish who became resentful of England's control over their country. One of these was Henry Grattan, who led 'the Patriots', arguing for a more favourable trading relationship with England, especially repeal of the Navigation Acts, which levied tariffs on goods leaving Ireland for England but not the other way around.

PREVIOUS PAGES:
IRISH REBELLION (1798)
The 1798 Irish rebellion saw Belfast Presbyterians and Catholics in the rest of the country united under the Society of United Irishmen banner. Both objected to Anglican rule from London, and were supported by a force from France, until the revolt was put down.

RIGHT:
UNITED IRISH BADGE
This is the emblem of the Society of United Irishmen. Influenced by the French Revolution, it includes the word 'equality' but contains an Irish harp.

OPPOSITE:
'THE PIKEMEN'
This sculpture commemorates the United Irish insurgents who overwhelmed Crown forces at Wexford in 1798, resulting in them abandoning the town. It was created by sculptor Eamonn O'Doherty.

BELOW:
BATTLE OF VINEGAR HILL (1798)
This battle saw the Crown forces led by Gerard Lake defeat the United Irishmen under Anthony Perry in County Wexford. It brought to an end the rebellion of the United Irishmen, and the Act of Union in 1800 then created the United Kingdom of Great Britain and Ireland.

WILLIAM THEOBALD WOLFE TONE.

ABOVE:
UNITED IRISHMEN REBELLION MEMORIAL
In the 1798 Irish rebellion, Glenmalure, in the Wicklow Mountains, was a stronghold of Michael Dwyer and his comrades. Today a commemoration stone, placed in 1998, marks it as a location that fostered rebellion. Two centuries earlier, Glenmalure had been the site of Fiac McHugh O'Byrne's taking up of arms against the invading English.

OPPOSITE:
WOLF TONE
Like Henry Grattan, Wolfe Tone was a Protestant who saw that uniting with Irish Catholics was the best way forward for Ireland, freeing it from being governed by Westminster. From Dublin, he helped to form the Society of United Irishmen.

FREE TRADE

In 1782, free trade was granted and instrumental in this were the Irish Volunteers, who were up to 100,000 strong and staged armed demonstrations in favour of Grattan's proposals.

As a result of the free trade, Ireland saw an economic boom in the 1780s, with canals built westward from Dublin. Much of the architecture of central Dublin stems from the eighteenth century.

In 1793, Catholics regained the right to vote and buy freehold land. Two years later the Orange Order was founded in County Armagh, to protect the interests of Ulster Protestants. Its name was a tribute to William of Orange.

IRISH REBELLION AND ACT OF UNION

In 1798 there was an Irish rebellion, led by the Society of United Irishmen, which had been formed in Belfast by Presbyterians. Led by Irish Protestant republican Wolfe Tone, the rebellion was supported by France, who landed troops in Mayo and then also sent ships to Donegal, where they were defeated in a naval battle.

The subsequent 1800 Acts of Union brought Ireland completely under the governance of the London parliament, and 1 January 1801 saw the creation of the United Kingdom of Great Britain and Ireland.

RELIGIOUS DIVIDE

By the beginning of the nineteenth century, then, the main political and religious groupings that we know today had begun to crystallize. After union between some Protestant and Catholic republicans in the eighteenth century – fighting together to take control of Ireland – the quelling of the rebellion from Westminster, in which 30,000 people died, had redrawn the map of allegiances within Ireland.

In the nineteenth century, under Daniel O'Connell, Irish republicans would come

almost exclusively from a Catholic base, with the Presbyterians largely abandoning the cause. Protestants mainly allied themselves with the Union, seeing Westminster as their best bet to represent their interests.

ABOVE:
THE LAST PARLIAMENT OF IRELAND
From 1297, there had been a parliament for Ireland, but with the Act of Union in 1800, there would be no need for decisions to be made in Dublin. This illustration shows Parliament House on College Green.

OPPOSITE:
DANIEL O'CONNELL
Daniel O'Connell was twice elected to the new United Kingdom parliament. He succeeded in having the bars on Catholics from higher offices of state and the judiciary lifted, the first in a series of moves throughout the 19th century that put Catholics on a more equal footing to Protestants than they had previously been.

REPRESENTATION IN WESTMINSTER

In 1832, as England and Wales saw the introduction of parliamentary representation that better reflected the make-up of the nations compared with the aristocracy-skewed previous system, so Ireland also had its Reform Act passed in Westminster. Since 1801, Ireland had had 100 seats at Westminster, but this was increased in 1832 and Catholics were now allowed to be members of parliament, as long as they had £10 worth of property. The change was partly down to Daniel O'Connell, who won a seat at Westminster representing Clare.

However, despite the progress being made for Catholics, a disaster was about to strike that would shape not just the future of Ireland and Britain, but also much of the world. The Great Irish Famine of 1845–49 would lead to mass starvation and emigration, meaning that the Irish would come to populate much of North America, Australasia and other parts of Britain on an unprecedented level. And the people the famine would hit most severely would be Ireland's peasant class – its Catholics.

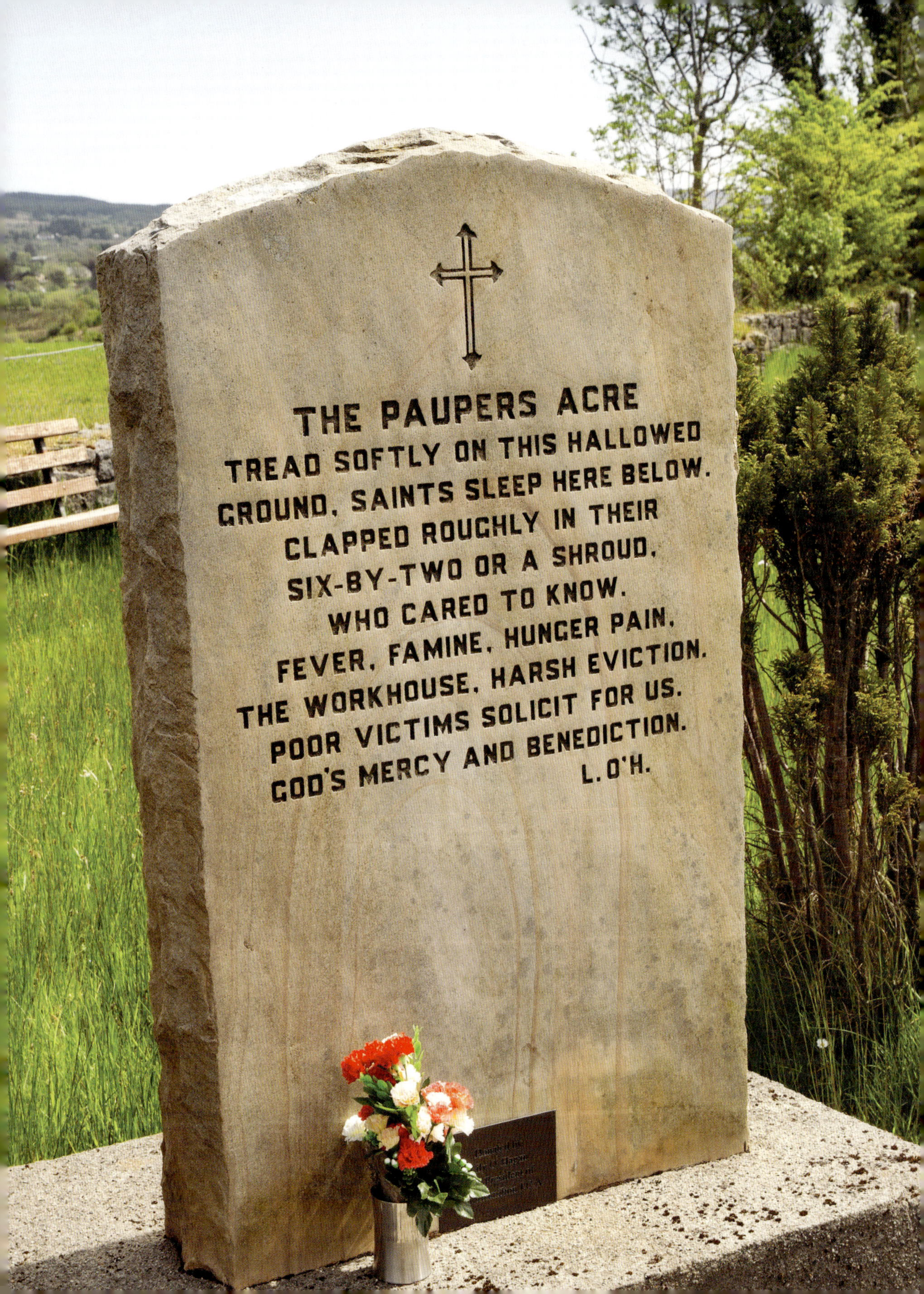
THE PAUPERS ACRE
TREAD SOFTLY ON THIS HALLOWED
GROUND, SAINTS SLEEP HERE BELOW.
CLAPPED ROUGHLY IN THEIR
SIX-BY-TWO OR A SHROUD,
WHO CARED TO KNOW.
FEVER, FAMINE, HUNGER PAIN,
THE WORKHOUSE, HARSH EVICTION.
POOR VICTIMS SOLICIT FOR US.
GOD'S MERCY AND BENEDICTION.
L. O'H.

FAMINE AND EMIGRATION

The lot of Catholics in Ireland improved politically in the first half of the nineteenth century. As well as being able to vote in Westminster elections, they were also allowed to be members of parliament. The gains were hard-won. Prime minister William Pitt the Younger resigned in protest when King George III blocked his attempt to repeal the Test Act, which discriminated against Catholics and nonconformist Protestants in various ways, including not allowing them to be employed by the state.

But, in 1829, prime minister Arthur Wellesley – the Dublin-born Napoleonic War hero and first Duke of Wellington, who had also been chief secretary for Ireland – saw more success with the Roman Catholic Relief Act, which allowed Catholics into the higher offices of the judiciary and the state. But, again, the prime minister had to threaten to resign to see the bill through. George IV eventually succumbed.

POTATO BLIGHT

However, all that was to pale into insignificance when compared with how a potato blight called *phytophthora infestans* would unleash mass starvation and death among the peasant, mainly Catholic, class of Ireland, and precipitate emigration on an unprecedented scale that would shape many countries of the New World – and some of the Old.

The disease that rotted Ireland's potatoes – which had become a staple food there – was first noticed in North America. In 1843 and 1844, it destroyed potato crops in the eastern

OPPOSITE:
PAUPERS' ACRE
Stones such as this, commemorating those who died with no means, many in the Great Irish Famine, are called paupers' acres. This one is in the town of Manorhamilton in County Leitrim. Manorhamilton was badly affected by the famine and graveyards were built to cope with the deaths.

United States. It was imported to Ireland when potatoes were carried by ships east across the Atlantic.

When the 1845 crop was harvested that October, it was revealed that up to half of it had been lost. The next year the figure was three-quarters of the crop.

Ireland had become dependent on the potato as a food source because, after being imported from America, it had been found to grow quickly with high yields in small areas. It replaced the previous staples of oats, wheat and barley, which had been cooked as porridge or bread, eaten with butter and milk.

EARLY RELIEF EFFORTS

In November 1845, Daniel O'Connell – along with other prominent Dubliners – raised the failure of the crop with the lord lieutenant of Ireland, Lord Heytesbury. They suggested opening Ireland's ports to foreign cereals, stopping distillation from grain, banning food exports and providing employment through public works. Lord Heytesbury said they 'were premature' and urged them not to be alarmed.

But prime minister Robert Peel bought £100,000 of cornmeal secretly from America. However, poor weather meant the first shipment did not arrive until February 1846 and, when it did, many Irish mills were not equipped to turn it into flour. He also set up a programme of public works for Ireland.

Peel repealed the Corn Laws – measures that had put tariffs on cereal imports – to try to alleviate the situation, which split the Tory party and caused the downfall of his government.

THE GREAT FAMINE

The incoming Whig administration – believers in free-market *laissez-faire* economics – stopped food aid and replaced the works programme with their own, insisting that the Irish could buy food from their public works wages. But the large scheme, involving half a million people, proved difficult to administer.

LEFT:
STARVING FAMILY
Some of the eyewitness accounts of what the famine did to people are heartbreaking. Cork magistrate Nicholas Cummins wrote of seeing "six famished and ghastly skeletons, to all appearances dead" lying on "filthy straw".

OPPOSITE:
KING GEORGE III
Under George III's reign, from 1760 to 1820, the Act of Union came into force, which brought together the kingdoms of England, Wales, Scotland and Ireland into one entity.

FAMINE
This 1997 memorial to the famine by sculptor Rowan Gillespie stands on Custom House Quay in Dublin. Similar figures stand in Ireland Park, Toronto, in Canada. Both depict people leaving their homeland to escape hunger.

LAND GRAB

In 1847, the British government decreed that Irish landowners should shoulder the bulk of the responsibility for feeding the starving and, as part of changes to the Irish Poor Laws, anyone with more than a quarter of an acre of land was prohibited from receiving relief. The result was that tens of thousands had to vacate their land to qualify for the relief – 90,000 in 1849 and 104,000 in 1850.

Thousands of debt-stricken landlords also sold their holdings, which were then bought by British speculators, who subsequently raised the rents for their tenant farmers, driving more from the land, many through eviction. In 1849 and 1850, 50,000 families were evicted, and larger farms under British ownership evolved. As in Scotland, smallholdings were amalgamated into bigger units, making land more economically productive, but breaking the bond between the land and those who had worked it for generations.

OPPOSITE:
WILLIAM PITT
William Pitt the Younger was prime minister at the time of the Act of Union and thought that there would be better relations between England and Ireland if the latter was part of a united kingdom.

BELOW:
BLIGHTED POTATO
The blight devastated Ireland's potato crop, upon which many agricultural communities relied. After Ireland's famine in the mid-19th century, there were potato blights – phytophthora infestans – in Germany and East Africa.

There has been much debate over whether the British government let the famine play out as it did to suit its own ends. Charles Trevelyan, who administered the government relief, admitted that having hard-up Irish landlords sell to investors – who would then implement changes to agriculture in Ireland – would be of benefit to Britain.

EMIGRATION

At least a million people are believed to have emigrated because of the famine. Ireland had been seeing its people leave since the mid-eighteenth century, as opportunities for better lives emerged in Britain's colonies. But the famine produced a severe spike in emigration numbers.

Certain areas were particularly favoured by migrants. Of the British mainland cities that the Irish moved to, looking for work, Liverpool stood out. By 1851, at least a quarter of the city's population was Irish-born. Liverpool even elected an Irish nationalist as an MP from 1885 to 1929. Further afield, the 1851 census in Toronto revealed that more than half of the city's population was Irish – in 1847, 38,000 Irish arrived in a city of only 20,000. And by 1850, the Irish made up a quarter of the population in Boston, New York City, Philadelphia and Baltimore.

PREVIOUS PAGES:
CARRICKSHOCK MASSACRE
At the Carrickshock Massacre of 14 December 1831, Catholic tenant farmers in Kilkenny confronted the Irish Constabulary. As a result, 17 people were killed. The issue that caused the tragedy was the withholding of tithes that the farmers had to pay to the Church of Ireland.

ABOVE:
FATHER MATTHEW
Father Theobald Matthew, from Tipperary, was a Catholic priest and teetotalist reformer, who founded the Catholic Total Abstinence Society. In the 1840s, more than half the adult population of Ireland had signed up, and he was seen as a benevolent presence during the famine.

OVERLEAF:
EMIGRATING
All classes of Irish saw better opportunities abroad in the 19th and 20th centuries. This picture, from 1930, shows Irish arrivals at Ellis Island in New York with their servants, having disembarked from the cruise ship *Queen Mary*.

NED KELLY
In the 19th century, the growing numbers of emigrants from Ireland made their mark on the Americas and Australasia. In Australia, Ned Kelly was an outlaw of Irish stock – his father, from Tipperary, had been deported for stealing two pigs, and his mother, from County Antrim, had emigrated as a child with her family.

DEPOPULATION

An 1841 census recorded 8.2 million people in Ireland; one 10 years later recorded 6.6 million. Families had starved to death and disease had ravaged those weakened by malnutrition. Many of those who had survived the famine had emigrated.

There was already resentment among a great swathe of the population towards the governing British before the 1840s, but the handling of the famine exacerbated this, especially because grain continued to be exported from Ireland at a time when so many of its people were starving.

The particularly wet summer of 1845 had caused excellent conditions for the spread of the potato blight. In the following drier summers, the blight disappeared. But the famine was to live long in the collective Irish memory – among those who stayed but also among those who emigrated.

THE 'IRISH QUESTION'

And it would crystallize what the British prime minister had called the 'Irish Question' in 1844, just before the famine struck. 'You have a starving population, an absentee aristocracy and an alien Church, and in addition the weakest executive in the world.' What would happen to a land that had been so put upon, and had to contend with these circumstances?

OPPOSITE:
ARRIVING IN NEW YORK
An Irish emigrant shields his eyes to glimpse New York City across the harbour from the arrivals point at Ellis Island. By the end of the 19th century, New York had become the largest urban Irish settlement in the world.

BELOW:
ONE FAMILY'S JOURNEY
A 1926 photo from New York showing the McKessy family, from Limerick, after arriving on the SS *Aurania*. Of the family's 21 children, 14 emigrated to America, five died and two stayed in Ireland.

INDEPENDENCE MOVEMENTS AND CIVIL WAR

Appropriately for somewhere that has the word 'land' in its name, land ownership has been central to the fortunes – and struggles – of Ireland. In the nineteenth century, about 10,000 English families owned practically all the farmland in Ireland, and rarely visited the acreage they owned. Centuries of legislation against Catholics had meant that, generally, the rural Irish – even if their families had previously been landowners – were now tenant farmers.

In 1868, William Gladstone was elected as the first Liberal British prime minister, with 'justice for Ireland' as part of his ticket. In 1870 the Landlord and Tenant (Ireland) Act was passed, which gave tenant farmers in Ireland more security of tenure, and rights to compensation if they were evicted. He also passed the Irish Church Act of 1869, which disestablished the Church of Ireland and separated it from the Church of England.

IRISH NATIONAL LAND LEAGUE

However, Gladstone and the Liberals were voted out in 1874 in favour of the Conservatives and, in 1879, the Irish National Land League – which united tenant farmers to fight in their interests – was formed. It was led by MP Charles Stewart Parnell, of the Home Rule Party, which had been established in 1873 to campaign for Ireland to rule itself but still within the United Kingdom.

The Land League did not encourage violence, but there was an increase in rural civil disobedience, such as rent strikes, in this period. The Land League's 'Land War' demanded the 'Three Fs' – fair rent, fixity of tenure and

OPPOSITE:
ATTACK ON THE FOUR COURTS
An attack in 1922 on the Four Courts building in Dublin – housing the Supreme Court, the Court of Appeal, the High Court and the Dublin Circuit Court – by opponents of the Anglo-Irish Treaty ignited the Irish Civil War.

free sale of land. This manifested itself particularly in resistance to evictions and withholding of rent.

In 1882, Parnell expanded the remit of the Land League to form the Irish National League, which also campaigned for home rule.

In the 1885 election, Parnell found himself – as leader of the Irish Parliamentary Party, which was the successor to the Home Rule League – holding the balance of power at Westminster, with 86 seats.

GOVERNMENT OF IRELAND BILL

With Parnell's support, Gladstone could form a government. The Liberals subsequently introduced the Government of Ireland Bill, which intended to create a devolved assembly for Ireland.

Ireland's Unionists and the Orange Order of Northern Ireland strongly opposed the Bill, saying that home rule was 'Rome Rule' – a Catholic majority ruling Ireland to the detriment of Protestants. Gladstone excluded the likes of Parnell from the drafting of the bill, and Parnell had mixed emotions towards it.

BELOW:
GLADSTONE'S CABINET, 1868
The English Liberal Party leader William Gladstone was predisposed towards greater freedoms for Catholics in Ireland and he won the 1868 General Election proposing the disestablishment of the Church of Ireland.

OPPOSITE:
LAND WAR
The 'land wars' of the late 19th and early 20th centuries involved tenant farmers withholding rent on a widespread basis in order to try to achieve better terms. The poster refers to leading backers of a better deal for tenant farmers, the imprisoned Charles Stewart Parnell and John Dillon.

THE LAND WAR!

NO RENT!

NO LANDLORDS GRASSLAND

Tenant Farmers, now is the time. Now is the hour. You proved false to the first call made upon you.

REDEEM YOUR CHARACTER NOW.

NO RENT

UNTIL THE SUSPECTS ARE RELEASED.

The man who pays Rent (whether an abatement is offered or not) while PARNELL, DILLON &c., are in Jail, will be looked upon as a Traitor to his Country and a disgrace to his class.

No RENT, No Compromise, No Landlords' Grassland, Under any ciroumstances.

Avoid the Police, and listen not to spying and deluding Bailiffs.

NO RENT! LET THE LANDTHIEVES DO THEIR WORST!

THE LAND FOR THE PEOPLE!

The bill was narrowly defeated. A number of Liberals who had voted against it broke away from the Liberals and merged with the Conservatives to form the Conservative and Unionist Party.

The Liberal Unionists were largely drawn from the Liberals' Whig faction. The Whigs had led several governments and were more aligned with the British establishment. Also, some of the Unionists held large estates in Ireland, which they feared would be broken up or confiscated if Ireland had its own government. Furthermore, Lord Frederick Cavendish – who, as chief secretary to Ireland, was killed in 1882 by Irish nationalists – had been the brother of the Liberal Unionists' leader Lord Hartington.

OPPOSITE:
WILLIAM GLADSTONE
William Gladstone saw Irish Home Rule through a moral lens – he believed in it so much that he spent much of his career trying to achieve it. But, ultimately, his quest was to split his Liberal Party.

BELOW:
EVICTIONS
The Irish National Land League encouraged willing tenant farmers to stop paying the rent their landlords demanded, proposing what they viewed as fairer rents. This led to many attempted evictions.

PLAN OF CAMPAIGN

In 1886, Irish farmers started their Plan of Campaign. Under this, tenants who felt overburdened by rent would pay a reduced rate to the League, who would hold on to it until the landlord agreed to accept the lesser rent.

FIGHT BETWEEN THE POLICE AND NATIONAL LAND LEAGUE SUPPORTERS

The period of violence involving the National Land League lasted from 1879 to 1882. The police – the Royal Irish Constabulary – were called upon to evict tenants who refused to pay their rent. Out of the National Land League came the Irish National League, under Charles Stewart Parnell, which campaigned on broader issues, such as Irish Home Rule. It is estimated that about a third of Land League activists were Catholic priests.

To clamp down on the unrest caused by the Plan of Campaign, the Conservatives introduced the Criminal Law and Procedure (Ireland) Act in 1887, which targeted the intimidation and unlawful assembly that came with conspiring to withhold agreed rents. This act resulted in the imprisonment of hundreds of people and more than 20 MPs, including Parnell.

PARNELL

It was Parnell's exploits that were to overshadow further attempts at Irish Home Rule. In 1889 he was cited in divorce papers by his former fellow Irish MP William O'Shea, and it was revealed in court that he had been in a long-term relationship with O'Shea's wife Katharine and had fathered three of her children.

The Irish National League defended him but Dublin's Roman Catholic Archbishop, William Joseph Walsh, condemned him, as did the nonconformist Protestants that made up much of the Liberal Party's support. The alliance with the Liberals collapsed, and Parnell's own party split between those who stood by him and those who did not.

DEATH OF PARNELL

Parnell married Katharine in 1891 but had kidney disease and died later that year of pneumonia. He was 45. Though he was an Anglican, Parnell's funeral was at the Irish national nondenominational Glasnevin Cemetery in Dublin. More than 200,000 people attended. In 1893, Gladstone introduced another home rule bill, which was passed by the House of Commons but not by the House of Lords, which at the time had a power of veto on bills.

BELOW & OPPOSITE:
CHARLES STEWART PARNELL
Charles Stewart Parnell was an inspirational leader who drew crowds, such as here at an anti-rent meeting in Limerick in 1879. He was to die only 12 years later, aged 45, after a scandal that ended his political career.

DERRY AUCHRIM

HOME RULE?

Home rule was dead in its tracks again but demands for it continued throughout the 1890s. The British government sought to quell some of the discontent and bring Ireland more in line with the Union by passing the Local Government (Ireland) Act in 1898. This modelled Irish counties on how they were administered in England, Wales and Scotland, with representatives elected locally to make decisions on behalf of areas. This system had developed on the British mainland throughout the nineteenth century, but in Ireland counties were still run by grand juries made up of major landowners.

Now nationalists could be voted in to run local affairs democratically, and John Redmond, who took over the pro-Parnell wing of the Irish Parliamentary Party after the Katharine O'Shea scandal, argued that this democratization of counties would stimulate calls for home rule, not quell them. He would be proved right.

PREVIOUS PAGES:
IRISH HOME RULE BILL
William Gladstone unveiled the Irish Home Rule Bill in 1886 and it was met with demonstrations and violence in Belfast, where the Protestant majority feared they would become second-class citizens in a Dublin-ruled Catholic Ireland.

OPPOSITE:
PHOENIX PARK MURDERS
In 1882, the Chief Secretary for Ireland and the Permanent Under-Secretary were murdered in Phoenix park, Dublin, by a Republican organisation called the Irish National Invincibles, a breakaway group from the Irish Republican Brotherhood.

LAND PURCHASE

In 1900, Redmond was elected the new leader of the reunited Irish Parliamentary Party and in 1902 the Land Conference in Dublin, forged by nationalist William O'Brien, led to a settlement between some major landlords and representatives of tenants. This was followed by the Land Purchase (Ireland) Act in 1903, passed by the Conservatives. Under this, tenants could

RIGHT:
WILLIAM GLADSTONE PRESENTING THE FIRST IRISH HOME RULE BILL
In June 1886, William Gladstone spent three hours presenting the case for Irish Home Rule to the Westminster Parliament. He beseeched his fellow MPs to grant Ireland home rule rather than be compelled to do it at a later date, in humiliation. The Bill was defeated by 30 votes.

BATTERING RAM USED FOR AN EVICTION

Extreme measures were used to evict tenant farmers from land and homes for which they had not paid rent. Tenant farmer Tom Bermingham had been withholding rent from the Vandeleur Estate in County Clare when a battering ram was used to break into his home in 1888. Present were those enforcing the eviction, but also those reporting on proceedings for the Land League.

buy their land and the government would pay the difference between the price they wanted to pay and the price the landlord demanded. It was part of the Conservatives' plan, as their Irish Secretary Gerald Balfour said in 1895, to 'kill home rule by kindness'.

The Act resulted in a rush of landlords seeking to sell and tenants to buy.

In 1906 the Liberals were returned to power, but this time without Gladstone, who had died in 1898, and without a desire to give Ireland home rule. However, after the 1910 general election, the Irish Parliamentary Party under John Redmond held the balance of power in the House of Commons. The prime minister, Herbert Asquith, came to an agreement with Redmond that Asquith would introduce a new home rule bill if Redmond supported him in his desire to reduce the power of the Lords, allowing them only to delay, not veto.

THE HOME RULE ACT

The 1911 Parliament Act was passed and the following year, another home rule bill was introduced. It was appropriate that the two went hand in hand, as the House of Lords had killed off the 1893 attempt at home rule, a power they now no longer had.

The Orange Order and Ulster Unionists were again determined not to let Ireland be run from Dublin, and the Orange and Unionist volunteers merged into the Ulster Volunteers, gathering arms to prepare for military action. This was followed by the formation of the Irish Volunteers in the south, also prepared

OPPOSITE:
KATHARINE O'SHEA
Katharine O'Shea was the English woman whose relationship with Charles Stewart Parnell lead to his political downfall. Parnell was named in divorce papers issued by Katharine's estranged husband, William O'Shea, who, like Parnell, was also an Irish Nationalist MP.

RIGHT:
JOHN REDMOND
John Redmond led the Irish Parliamentary Party after the death of Charles Stewart Parnell, the party's founder. As an MP, he saw the Irish Home Rule Act finally pass through Parliament in 1914, although the outbreak of World War I delayed it being enacted, before the 1916 Easter Rising saw less patient Nationalists try to force matters.

to physically fight – for home rule. The Home Rule Act was given royal assent on 18 September 1914, but was immediately suspended because the previous month Britain had declared war on Germany after its failure to withdraw its troops from Belgium, in what was to be the start of World War I.

John Redmond encouraged Irishmen to volunteer for the British war effort, in the hope that a quick victory would enable the government to enact home rule. But victory was not to be quick.

EASTER MONDAY

On 24 April 1916 – Easter Monday – members of the Irish Volunteers led by Patrick Pearse joined James Connolly's Irish Citizen Army, and 200 women from the Irishwomen's Council, and seized strategically important buildings in Dublin, such as a telegraph station and court buildings. They proclaimed Ireland's independence from the United Kingdom, with Pearse reading out the statement outside Dublin's General Post Office. What became known as the Easter Rising sparked similar attempts to take control of towns across Ireland.

The British army responded by sending thousands of troops and a gunboat to Dublin, and bombarded the rebels' positions in Dublin city centre with artillery. With their superior numbers and equipment, the British crushed the rising and Pearce surrendered on Saturday 29 April. The British took 3500 people prisoner and Pearse and 14 other leaders, including Connolly, were executed. After 50 years of attempts at home rule by constitutional means, violence had returned to Ireland's quest for self-determination – and was met with greater violence.

FAILED WAR DRAFT

In early 1918, with Britain running low on troops to fight World War I, the government announced that it intended to draft Irishmen, who until then had been exempt. The backlash was furious, as shown in the result of the December 1918 general election, after the war had concluded. Sinn Fein – a Republican party founded in 1905 that had become the home of the surviving rebels from the 1916 Easter Rising – won three-quarters of the seats in Ireland.

And they were not going to play the Westminster parliamentary game that Redmond and Parnell had done. On 21 January 1919, their 27 MPs assembled in Dublin and declared sovereignty over the whole island

– all 32 counties. On that same day, members of the Irish Volunteers ambushed two policemen escorting a consignment of gelignite explosives at Soloheadbeg, County Tipperary. The two members of the Royal Irish Constabulary (RIC) were killed and their weapons and explosives stolen. Two years of violence were to follow – as the British used force to attempt to resist the creation of the breakaway state – and the Soloheadbeg assault is often seen as the first engagement in the Irish War of Independence.

OPPOSITE:
PATRICK PEARSE
Patrick Pearse, a member of the Irish Republican Brotherhood, was one of the instigators of the Easter Rising. Along with 15 other rebels he was executed for it. He was also a notable writer, penning poems and plays in English and Irish.

WAR OF INDEPENDENCE

Throughout 1919, the Volunteers – who started to become called the Irish Republican Army (IRA) – attempted to capture weaponry and to free Republican prisoners, as well as ambushing RIC and British Army patrols, and attacking barracks. Meanwhile, the British government bolstered the RIC with recruits from Britain, such as, from 1920, the Black and Tans, mostly former World War I soldiers from England, Wales and Scotland, whose name derives from the improvised uniforms they initially wore.

BELOW:
ULSTER VOLUNTEERS
This picture shows Ulster Volunteers meeting regular British troops in Omagh, County Tyrone. The Ulster Volunteers, with their distinctive headgear, were formed in 1912 to oppose Irish Home Rule from Dublin.

LEFT:
IRISH REPUBLICAN ARMY
Leader of Sinn Fein Eamon de Valera inspecting the Western Division of the Irish Republican Army in County Clare in 1921, when he was a fugitive from the British. The army had formed in 1917 from the Irish Volunteers and Irish Citizen Army to fight for independence.

OPPOSITE:
BLACK AND TANS
This photograph shows one of the Black and Tans on duty in Dublin. The Black and Tans – so-called because of the colour of their uniforms – were a division of constables established to try to maintain British rule in the Irish War of Independence, from 1919 to 1921. Many of the members were former British soldiers who had fought in World War I.

BELOW:
HOGAN'S FLYING COLUMN
Sean Hogan was a leader of the 3rd Tipperary Brigade of the Irish Republican Army during the War of Independence and his 'flying column' – a mobile unit of men – that became active in the county in January 1921.

IRISH VOLUNTEERS
A group of the Irish Volunteers, which had formed in 1913. With the Ulster Volunteers having formed in 1912 and there being tensions over the future of Ireland with regard to Home Rule, the Irish Volunteers grew in number to 200,000 by mid-1914. In September that year, the force split over Irish parliamentary leader John Redmond's commitment to the British World War I effort.

ULSTER VOLUNTEERS' EQUIPMENT
Ulster Volunteers photographed with Boer War-era British Army equipment at Larne, County Antrim. In 1913 the Volunteers became the Ulster Volunteer Force. Other equipment for the UVF was to come from Germany, just before the outbreak of World War I.

Ten thousand men enlisted for the Black and Tans during the War of Independence, and they gained a reputation for brutality and carrying out reprisal attacks on civilians and civilian property, further swaying the Irish population against British rule.

Alongside the Black and Tans were the Auxiliaries, a division of the RIC consisting of former British army officers.

The guerrilla conflict also involved civil disobedience, such as the refusal of Irish railwaymen to transport British forces or military supplies.

EDWARD CARSON
Edward Carson, a Dublin-born Anglican, founded the Ulster Volunteers to try to make sure Home Rule was not achieved. A barrister by trade, he was a committed Unionist but one who also was uneasy with much of Unionist culture in Ulster, such as that of the Orange Order. An Irish speaker, in his youth he had been a keen player of Gaelic sports. He is pictured here inspecting a parade of his Volunteers in 1914.

EASTER RISING
The Easter Rising of 1916 saw Republican forces command the streets of Dublin, where they were opposed by British troops (pictured). Like the Ulster Volunteers, many of the Republicans' arms were sourced from Germany. In 1914, the novelist and revolutionary Erskine Childers had travelled to Germany to source rifles.

In June 1920 – in elections administered by the United Kingdom – Republicans won control of most of the county councils, and the British found they had no authority in south and west Ireland.

CONFLICT DEEPENS

By late 1920, 300 people had been killed in the war, but then the violence escalated. On 21 November, 14 British intelligence operatives were assassinated and then the RIC fired on the crowd at a Gaelic football match, killing 14 and wounding 65.

Before the month was out, the IRA killed 17 Auxiliaries in the village of Kilmichael in County Cork. Britain declared martial law in much of southern Ireland and burned out the centre of Cork city in reprisal for an ambush.

Meanwhile, in Ulster, loyalists were conducting reprisals on the Catholic population for IRA activities. In July 1920 they drove 8000 mostly Catholic workers out of the Belfast shipyards. During the whole conflict, more than 500 people were killed in Belfast and 23,000 made homeless. Fifty thousand fled Belfast due to intimidation.

ABOVE:
KILMAINHAM GAOL
Kilmainham Gaol in Dublin was where members of the Easter Rising were executed by firing squad. Charles Stewart Parnell had been jailed there in the 19th century. It is now a museum.

OPPOSITE:
USE OF ROOFTOPS IN THE EASTER RISING
The Irish Citizen Army and Irish Volunteers made use of Dublin's rooftops as vantage points during the Easter Rising. Much of the fighting consisted of sniping and long-range gun battles, but the British also bombarded Irish positions with artillery.

PARTITION OF IRELAND

The division between Protestants and Catholics in Ulster was legitimized by the Irish Republic approving of the 'Belfast Boycott' of Unionist-owned businesses in the city, enforced by the IRA, who stopped trains and lorries and destroyed goods. And the difference between Ulster and the rest of Ireland was soon to become politically official, with the Government of Ireland Act being given royal assent in December 1920. This divided Ireland into two entities within the United Kingdom – the six northeastern counties forming Northern Ireland and the rest becoming Southern Ireland.

SINN FEIN

Sinn Fein President Eamon de Valera addresses a march to protest against continuing British rule in May 1918. The various Republican groups that had fought in the Easter Rising came together under the Sinn Fein banner in 1917 and in December 1918, Sinn Fein won 73 of the 105 Irish seats at the UK General Election, leading to them declaring themselves the democratic rulers of Ireland.

PHARMACEUTICAL &
CHEMISTS

RUINS OF CORK CITY CENTRE
The ruins of Cork city centre in December 1920 after the Royal Irish Constabulary Reserve Force set fires there in retaliation for IRA attacks. More than 40 business premises, 300 residential properties, the City Hall and Carnegie Library were destroyed by the fires, which were set by incendiary devices.

ANGLO-IRISH TREATY

On 11 July 1921, a truce was achieved. First, the British – under prime minister David Lloyd George – called off the policy of using house burnings for reprisals. The whole conflict was costing more and more in casualties and money and the force Britain was using was damaging its reputation among its electorate and abroad. The IRA leaders also knew that they did not have the resources to keep on fighting indefinitely.

The truce – and the subsequent Anglo-Irish Treaty – was to involve not only the personal involvement of King George V, but also that of the prime minister of South Africa, Jan Smuts. The king, who had let his unhappiness at the behaviour of the Black and Tans be known, sought Smuts's input for his speech to open the new parliament of Northern Ireland in Belfast. Smuts pushed the king to call for conciliation in Ireland, and he duly delivered such a speech, with Sinn Fein leader Eamon de Valera subsequently agreeing to talks with Lloyd George.

IRISH FREE STATE

What resulted was the creation of the Irish Free State as a dominion of the British Empire, but with its own parliament – the same status as Canada at the time. Northern Ireland chose not to be part of the Free State.

For the transition to Free State status, a provisional government was set up, under Michael Collins, who had been a government minister in the self-declared Irish Republic. But many members of Collins's Sinn Fein – and the IRA – saw the creation of the Free State and Northern Ireland as a betrayal of the Irish Republic and took up arms.

YORK STREET RIOTS
In the York Street riots in Belfast in 1920, Unionists attacked Catholic shipyard workers on the way to their jobs. Home Rule had been granted to Ireland, sparking the unrest in Belfast, in which 62 people were killed and more than 200 injured. As well as Loyalists attacking Catholic areas, there were reprisals in which Unionist communities and properties were targeted.

ABOVE:
THE AUXILIARIES
As fighting over who would rule Ireland and on what terms took place through 1921 during the War of Independence, the British unit the Auxiliaries were called upon. Like the Black and Tans, they were an offshoot of the Royal Irish Constabulary. Members are shown here after their base at the London and Northwest Hotel in Dublin was attacked in April 1921.

OPPOSITE:
MICHAEL COLLINS
During the War of Independence, Michael Collins was Director of Intelligence for the IRA and a minister in the self-declared Irish Republic.
He was then Chairman of the Provisional Government of the Irish Free State and commander-in-chief of the Irish National Army.
He supported the Anglo-Irish Treaty and was killed by anti-treaty forces in August 1922.

CIVIL WAR

Battles were fought between the new National Army and anti-treaty forces in June and July 1922 and Michael Collins was killed in an ambush in August. The British government supplied the National Army with weapons, vehicles and artillery to resist the rebellion. Anti-treaty forces took Cork, Limerick and Waterford, and proclaimed Munster a 'republic', but the better-equipped Free State took them all back, with the IRA badly split and lacking cohesion. Also, the Catholic Church had declared that it supported the Free State, deeming it the lawful government.

The civil war descended into particularly bitter acrimony when the Free Sate started to execute prisoners, including the London-born author and treaty negotiator Erskine Childers, who had been fighting on the anti-treaty side.

Finally, in February 1923, the Republican leader Liam Deasy was captured and called on his fellow combatants to lay down their arms.

LEGACY OF CONFLICT

One legacy of the civil war is the dominant political units that exist in the Republic of Ireland today: Fine Gael, which formed from pro-treaty supporters; Fianna Fail, which formed from anti-treaty supporters; and Sinn Fein, which was anti-treaty and anti-partition.

PREVIOUS PAGES:
BRITISH SNIPERS
British snipers take aim from a window in Sackville Street, Dublin, during the Irish Civil War in 1922. Although the war was fought between the Irish National Army and the anti-Anglo-Irish Treaty IRA, British forces remained in Dublin to ensure the implementation of the 1921 treaty.

RIGHT:
BIRTH OF THE IRISH REPUBLIC
Irish troops parade in Dublin to mark the birth of the Irish Republic on 18 April 1949. The day selected for the formal celebration of the severance of all ties with the British Commonwealth was the 33rd anniversary of the Easter Rising.

In 1932, Fianna Fail, with Eamon de Valera as leader, won the Free State's general election, and in 1937 De Valera supervised the writing of a new constitution for the dominion, renaming it Ireland (Eire in Irish).

BIRTH OF EIRE

Asserting its distance from Britain, Ireland remained neutral during World War II, although tens of thousands volunteered to serve in the British forces. And, in 1949, Ireland completed its journey of self-determination and formally left the Commonwealth, becoming a republic. The years following partition for Northern Ireland showed constant Unionist government within the United Kingdom, yet there was still a sizeable Catholic minority, who were discriminated against concerning the likes of jobs and housing.

While both Northern Ireland and Southern Ireland remained peaceful for the decades after the end of the Irish Civil War, the problem that had plagued the island for centuries – a large chunk of the population not having representation – remained in Ulster. And as the 20th century progressed, this imbalance would lead to more violence.

OVERLEAF:
LAND MARKER
An old World War II aerial land marker on the County Mayo coast at Downpatrick Head. Ireland was ostensibly neutral during the Second World War but only Allied forces had the codes for the 'Eire' markers to tell them where they were.

KENNEDY
Lemon's
PURE SWEETS
THE
ICE CREAM PARLOR
WATERPROOFERS

EIR
64

BRIDGES of DUBLIN

MODERN IRELAND

With the election in 1932 of Eamon de Valera and Fianna Fail, the people of what we now know as the Republic of Ireland had voted in a party that had opposed the Anglo-Irish Treaty. In that gesture, the road was set for the 26 counties to become fully independent of Britain. They already had their own elected government in Dublin and, as a dominion of the British Empire, like Australia or Canada, the land had little interference from Westminster.

The state's new constitution in 1937 created the roles of president and taoiseach – prime minister. As taoiseach, De Valera steered Ireland through World War II as a neutral country. However, behind the scenes Ireland aided Britain – sending firefighters to Northern Ireland when Belfast was bombed by German aircraft, and helping Britain decide when to launch D-Day by supplying weather reports.

LOOKING TO THE FUTURE

De Valera's government was also ruthless in clamping down on the activities of the IRA, even though the IRA had been the legitimate army when De Valera had become president of the Irish Republic in 1919. The IRA, which had been supplanted as the official defence force by the National Army, started a bombing campaign in Britain while the UK's attentions were focused on the war. Some IRA leaders also sought help from Nazi Germany; the Irish government interned all active IRA members and had several executed.

Despite not having suffered the ravages of World War II, Ireland emerged as a new republic with a still largely rural economy with little investment and a population that could often see that there were better lives on offer elsewhere.

OPPOSITE:
LIFFEY QUAYS
The Liffey Quays, along the north and south banks of the River Liffey in central Dublin, have been settled since the origins of the city in Viking times. They were developed during the time of King John and used as Dublin's port until the 1800s, when the water was deemed too shallow and the port was moved downstream.

THE INTERNATIONAL

BELFAST IN THE BLITZ
The Belfast Blitz consisted of four Luftwaffe raids in April and May 1941, killing more than 1,000 people. Particular targets were Belfast's shipyards and its factories. Nazi propagandist Lord Haw-Haw broadcast that there would be "Easter eggs for Belfast".

In 1958, Fianna Fail's Sean Lemass, as taoiseach, stated that the very future of Ireland as an independent state was at risk if there were no changes to the economy. Subsequently, investment in industrial infrastructure was boosted and tax incentives were given to foreign manufacturers to set up in Ireland. As a direct result, opportunities rose and emigration fell.

CATHOLIC DOMINATION

Although there had been free secondary education in Britain since the 1940s, it was not introduced in Ireland until 1967. Unlike in Britain, most schools in Ireland had been run by the Roman Catholic Church, which also controlled many of the country's hospitals.

OPPOSITE TOP:
DAMAGE FROM AN IRA BOMB ATTACK IN COVENTRY
In 1939 and 1940 the IRA carried out a series of attacks on the civil infrastructure of Britain in its S-Plan campaign, in objection to British troops being stationed in Northern Ireland. In August 1939 five people died after a bomb exploded in Coventry city centre.

OPPOSITE LOWER:
HAMMERSMITH BRIDGE ATTACK
Two policemen stand on Hammersmith Bridge in London after two IRA bombs were detonated there in March 1939. There were no casualties, but traffic was diverted away from the bridge for a month. In the same week, four more bombs exploded in Coventry.

BELOW:
BOMBING OF MIDLAND BANK, PARK LANE, LONDON
On the same day in June 1939, branches of Midland Bank, Westminster Bank and Lloyds Bank were targeted in a bombing campaign. Typical of S-Plan explosions, the bombs targeted one type of building simultaneously – public lavatories, railway stations, cinemas, post offices and post boxes experienced similar fates.

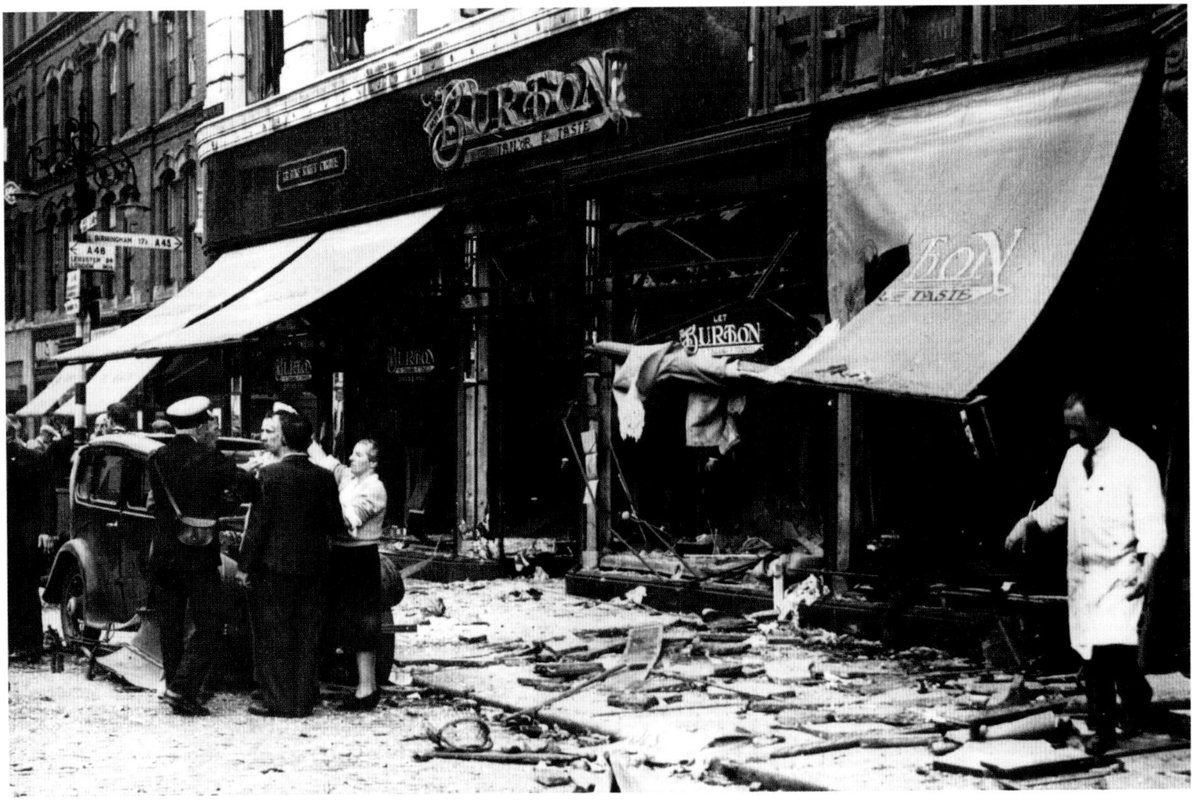
BURTON
TAILOR & TASTE
LET BURTON
A46
A45

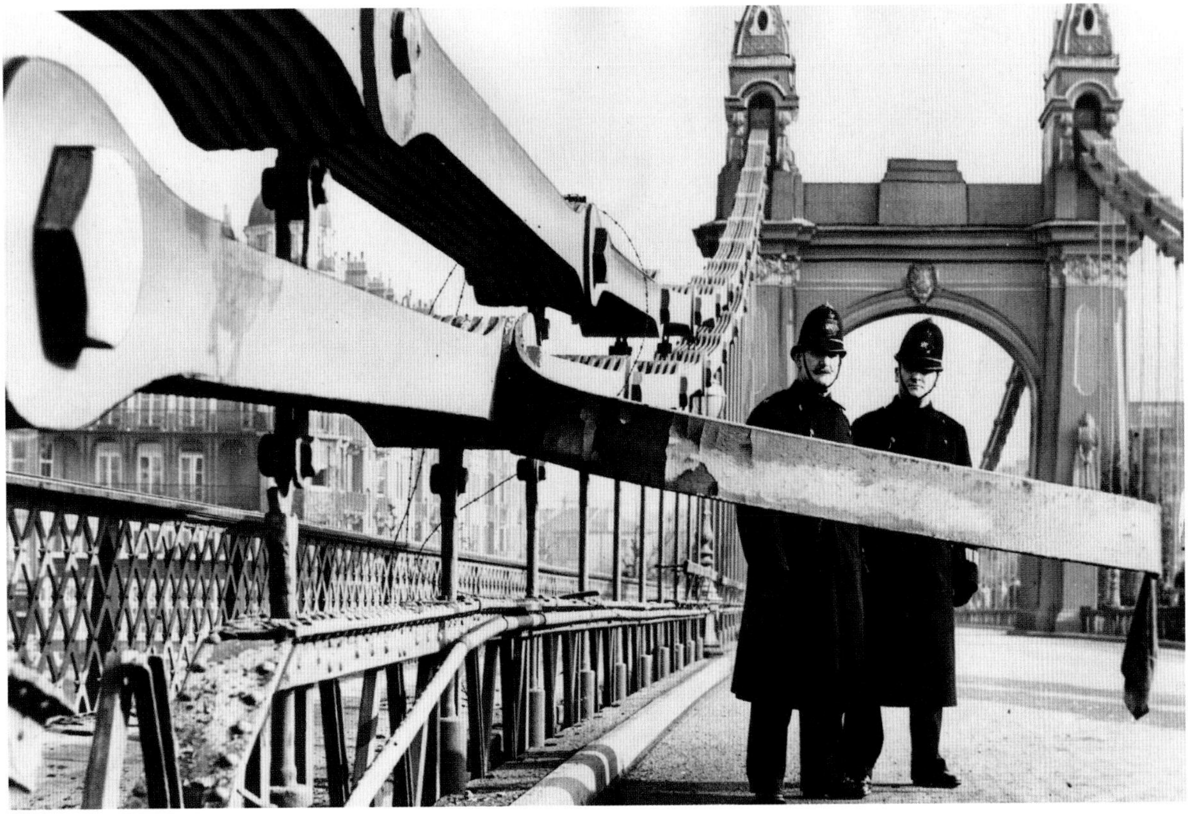

PEAT-CUTTING

Nine farmers help a tenth cut peat in the Republic of Ireland. Peat occurs widely in Ireland, and has been commonly used as fuel, although a prohibition order was introduced in 2022. In 1946 a state-owned company was put in charge of peat extraction.

The Church was central to many parts of Irish life – its objection to divorce and remarriage was part of state legislation and its views on pornography, abortion and contraception had also been similarly adopted.

Such was its power in twentieth-century Ireland that major publications freely available in other Western countries – such as *Playboy* and the British newspaper the *News of the World* – were only sanctioned in the Republic of Ireland towards the end of the century, as they were viewed as salacious. Similarly, Paul Raymond's pornographic magazines were not available until 2011. From its release in 1979, until 1987, the film *Monty Python's Life of Brian* was banned for being blasphemous, and there was even a moral objection to jazz which, in the 1930s, was banned for a short time from the radio.

SOCIAL CHANGE

At the same time as economic turmoil, the last decades of the twentieth century and first of the twenty-first saw great social change in Ireland, too. The Catholic Church's dominance over legislation waned, and divorce was legalized, homosexuality decriminalized and abortion allowed in limited cases.

The rulings on divorce and abortion were a victory for feminists, who had been campaigning for better rights for women in Ireland since the nineteenth century. In the 1870s, Anna Haslam and Isabella Tod had argued for women's suffrage. Women then played an active role in the 1916 Easter Rising, with voting rights activist Hannah Sheehy Skeffington saying: 'It is the only instance I know of in history when men fighting for freedom voluntarily included women.'

WOMEN'S RIGHTS

In 1922 the Irish Free State declared that women would have the same voting rights as men but, under the leadership of Eamon de Valera, Catholic doctrine became enshrined in law, so contraception and divorce were outlawed.

LEFT:
MARY ROBINSON
President Mary Robinson inspects a guard of honour after her inauguration in 1990 at St Patrick's Hall, Dublin Castle. She was president until 1997 and was the Republic of Ireland's first female president. Under her tenure, contraception was liberalised, homosexuality decriminalised and divorce legalised.

OPPOSITE:
LEGALISATION OF DIVORCE
A Fine Gael poster in 1995 encouraging people to vote in favour of legalising divorce. The 'Yes' vote won, although the Catholic Church urged people to vote 'No'. A referendum had previously rejected legalisation in 1986.

DAVID ALLEN
IF THIS WAS YOUR DAUGHTER,
YOU'D GIVE HER A SECOND CHANCE.
FG
FINE GAEL
VOTE
YES
NOV 24
GIVE SOMEONE YOU KNOW A SECOND CHANCE.

It wasn't until the 1970s that women gained more choice over their lives: in 1973 the law that denied married women the opportunity to work in the public sector was lifted, and, from 1979, contraceptives could be sold, on prescription.

In 1990, Mary Robinson was elected the first female president of the Republic, and Mary McAleese was president between 1997 and 2011. Women have been members of the Irish parliament in recent years in increasing numbers.

FEMALE FIRST MINISTERS

Such an about-turn has also happened regarding gender in politics in Northern Ireland. Michelle O'Neill became the province's first minister in 2024 and, before her, Arlene Foster held that position for two terms. But, being in the United Kingdom since partition, Northern Ireland had not experienced the greater restrictions on women's lives that the Republic had. Significant about Michelle O'Neill becoming first minister is that she is the first nationalist in Northern Ireland to do so – she represents Sinn Fein, which became the largest party in the Northern Ireland Assembly in 2022.

NORTHERN IRELAND – THE TROUBLES

When partition happened, James Craig, the first prime minister of Northern Ireland, had declared: 'We are a Protestant Parliament and a Protestant State.' And so the province was run, with the Catholic minority being denied access to better jobs and housing – in practice, if not in law. Sinn Fein always had a minority of the vote, but a period of change was to be ushered in – and it came hand in hand with violence. In 1968, the Northern Ireland Civil Rights Association, protesting over discrimination against Catholics, had a march suppressed by police, and the following year there were clashes with the police and Ulster loyalists.

1970S IRA

IRA members with guns during a training and propaganda exercise in 1977. In the 1970s and 1980s, the Republicans' fight for Ireland to be one nation claimed thousands of lives, with various nationalist forces using widespread violence to further their cause, and meeting with reprisals from the Ulster Volunteer Force.

2848 XI

STRIFE IN DERRY
Police using water cannon on the streets of Derry in 1969 during civil rights demonstrations in the Bogside. The mainly Catholic area of the Bogside is seen as the starting point of 'the Troubles', sparked by demonstrations for greater civil rights for Catholics. For large periods between 1969 and 1972, the Bogside became a no-go area for the police and British Army.

One way
At any time

OPPOSITE:
AFTERMATH OF RIOTS IN DERRY
The summer of 1969 saw civil rights demonstrations turn into riots on the streets of Derry. Part of Derry declared itself Free Derry, an Irish Nationalist area consisting mainly of the Bogside and Creggan areas. Barricades were erected to prevent the mainly Protestant Royal Ulster Constabulary from entering.

LEFT:
RIOTS IN BELFAST
A teenage civilian is arrested by two British soldiers on the streets of Belfast during a civil rights demonstration. Tension between the Catholic and Protestant communities saw the first 'peace line' erected there in September 1969, between the Catholic Falls and Protestant Shankhill communities.

BELOW:
RUC RIOT POLICE
Royal Ulster Constabulary police on the streets of Derry during a civil rights demonstration. For decades the RUC was seen as being staffed by Protestants and favouring them.

BRITISH MARKSMEN IN BELFAST
A British marksman takes aim at a suspect from an Army observation post on the roof of a council tower block in the Catholic area of New Lodge in Belfast in 1978. The terraced streets and tower blocks of New Lodge, immediately north of Belfast city centre, lie in the shadow of the city's Cave Hill.

The British government deployed troops to Northern Ireland, and 'peace walls' were erected between nationalist and loyalist neighbourhoods in Belfast, and other towns, to keep apart warring factions.

BLOODY SUNDAY

On Sunday 30 January 1972, British soldiers shot 26 unarmed civilians in Derry. This incident – Bloody Sunday – would be a pivotal moment in the Troubles, spurring recruitment for the IRA, and leaving a legacy that would encompass two public inquiries; spawn numerous songs, TV programmes and films; and lead to British prime minister David Cameron apologizing in 2010 for Britain's actions.

Bloody Sunday also sparked a bombing campaign by the IRA across Northern Ireland and England to try to force a united Ireland. The campaign went as far as attempting to assassinate British prime minister Margaret Thatcher in her hotel room at her party's conference in Brighton. These sectarian attacks were met with reprisals from loyalists, and over three decades more than 3500 people were killed in the Troubles.

SEEKING PEACE

In 1993, John Major's Westminster government secured agreements from nationalist leaders in Northern Ireland and the Republic of Ireland government for a change to the constitutions of Northern Ireland and the Republic that would let Ulster decide whether it wanted to remain in the Union or join a united Ireland. Loyalist leaders opposed this but further negotiations – and a change in unionist leadership, with David Trimble in charge – led to the Good Friday Agreement in 1998, in which nationalist and loyalist politicians agreed on a power-sharing way forward.

BLOODY SUNDAY MASSACRE
This picture was taken minutes before paratroopers opened fire on a group of demonstrators on 30 January 1972, in what became known as Derry's Bloody Sunday massacre.

J. QUINN

ABOVE:
ALDERSHOT BOMBING
In February 1972 a bomb exploded at the officers' mess at the British Army's 16th Parachute Brigade in Aldershot, Hampshire. The IRA said it was in retaliation for Bloody Sunday. Seven people were killed in the Aldershot blast, including a Catholic military chaplain. Nineteen people were injured. IRA member Noel Jenkinson was convicted and imprisoned for his part in the bombing.

OPPOSITE:
BRIGHTON BOMBING
Damage to the Grand Hotel, Brighton, where Conservative Party members, including Prime Minister Margaret Thatcher, were staying for their annual conference in October 1984. The hotel was targeted by a bomb that killed five people, including MP Anthony Berry. More than 30 people were injured.

GOOD FRIDAY PEACE AGREEMENT

Despite the 'Real IRA' puncturing the agreement with the single largest atrocity of the Troubles, its bombing of Omagh, which killed 29, the ceasefire largely held and, in 2005, Gerry Adams – the long-time Sinn Fein leader – called on IRA members to lay down their weapons.

The peace process officially ended in 2007 when the Democratic Unionist Party and Sinn Fein formed a government at Stormont, Northern Ireland's parliament. Sinn Fein, which, in Northern Ireland, had unashamedly been the political wing of the IRA, was now a mainstream political party; 15 years later, it would even have a majority in the Northern Ireland Assembly.

CAN PEACE LAST?

Between 1972 and 1999, Northern Ireland was under direct rule from Westminster, and the delicate truce between unionists and republicans in Northern Ireland has led to periods in which co-operation has broken down.

There are probably more difficulties in the years ahead. In the 2021 census the Catholic population of Northern Ireland was slightly larger than the Protestant population, because the birth rate among Catholics had been higher, as it has been traditionally.

The Gift Shop
CYCLES
CAR

OMAGH BOMBING
Debris left by the Omagh bombing of August 1998, carried out by the 'Real IRA', which opposed the Good Friday Agreement of that year. The bombing killed 29 people and injured more than 200 others – the deadliest incident of the Troubles in Northern Ireland. The Real IRA later apologised and said the bomb had not been intended to kill civilians.

And with a Sinn Fein first minister in Stormont and a large Sinn Fein presence in the Dublin parliament, it is probable that the issue of a united Ireland will return to the agenda, which is unlikely to please loyalists, who would fear that they would be a discriminated-against minority in a united Ireland, echoing the fears of 'Rome Rule' they had more than a century ago when home rule from Dublin was on the agenda for the island.

Many loyalists already feel betrayed by Britain, because Brexit drew a Customs Union border down the Irish Sea, putting Northern Ireland one step removed from the UK.

However, the 2021 census in Northern Ireland also showed a growth in numbers of people not aligning with either denomination, and the Alliance Party – which eschews sectarianism – has a sizeable minority; at the 2024 general election, it took 15 per cent of the votes cast in the province.

LANGUAGE: LEGACY OF IRELAND

While the Catholic Church had retained its power over Ireland, the Irish language had not fared so well. Ireland had started its life as a republic with English as its de facto first language (although Irish was still the official first language). Irish had been the dominant vernacular for centuries beforehand, with its own script – Ogham. But since the eighteenth century, Irish had been discouraged, with the English and Anglo-Irish ruling the land. And increasingly in the twentieth and twenty-first centuries, Irish as a first language became limited to people in pockets mostly in the west of Ireland, although it is used as a second language by many more.

The flipside of the Irish being forced to use English has been the host of Irish writers who have been lauded for their skill with words and

BELFAST MURALS
A Unionist mural in a Protestant Belfast area, one of many in the city. The murals – both in Catholic and Protestant areas – have become a feature of the city, and tours are taken by sightseers to visit them. This one celebrates the work of the Ulster Freedom Fighters.

UFF. 2ND. BATT. C COY
REEBOK
Reebok
adidas
McEWAN'S

story. Descended from a culture rich in folklore and storytelling, Oscar Wilde, Bram Stoker, James Joyce, W.B. Yeats, Samuel Beckett, C.S. Lewis and George Bernard Shaw put Ireland on the literary map in the nineteenth and twentieth centuries with their internationally recognized works.

RIVERDANCE

The twentieth century also saw the music and dance that is so much part of Irish culture find itself on the international stage. The phenomenon of Riverdance took Irish dancing worldwide from the 1990s and, before that, the booming American folk scene sparked an interest in Irish music – which much folk and country & western music drew on, the traditions having been exported by Irish immigrants.

Some Irish acts, such as The Chieftains and The Dubliners, found fame playing traditional music; others – such as Thin Lizzy, formed in Dublin, The Pogues, formed in London, and Belfast's Van Morrison – used Celtic influences in rock music. Ireland's biggest music act, U2, have become a global phenomenon through their music and hi-tech concerts. Bob Geldof, of Dublin's Boomtown Rats, also became particularly high-profile through his Band Aid and Live Aid ventures, raising money for the starving of Ethiopia in the 1980s.

Such personalities – and the large numbers of Irish people who have become household names through

OPPOSITE:
GEORGE BERNARD SHAW
Playwright George Bernard Shaw – best known for his play *Pygmalion*, turned into the musical *My Fair Lady* – was born in Dublin in 1856. He moved to London, and was awarded the Nobel Prize in Literature in 1925. As well as being seen as one of the leading playwrights of his generation, he was also a polemicist, with controversial views on subjects such as vaccination and eugenics.

LEFT:
C.S. LEWIS
The author of the *Narnia* books was born in Belfast and moved to England after being educated there from the age of nine. His Church of Ireland upbringing was to have a deep effect on him and, although he rejected God as a teenager, he returned to the church and his Christian views imbued his *Narnia* books.

JAMES JOYCE

James Joyce is recognised as one of the most influential writers of the twentieth century, especially in his novel *Ulysses*, with its use of stream of consciousness. Born in Dublin in 1882, he is also known for his short story collection *Dubliners*, specifically about life in the Irish capital.

film and TV – have cast the land of their birth in a different light from how the rest of the world had grown to view the country. For long seen by Britain as problematic and a land of conflict, a different Ireland was emerging.

TOURISM AND THE ARTS

And it was an Ireland that people wanted to visit. Now, tourism is one of the main drivers of the economy of the Republic of Ireland. City breaks are highly popular for people to take in the beautiful Georgian architecture of Dublin, dating from when the British were building it up as a provincial capital in the eighteenth and nineteenth centuries, as well as tours of the wild west coast. In particular, a heritage industry has grown up to show Ireland and its culture to those whose ancestors emigrated, and there is even a tourism industry based on the 'Troubles' in Belfast – its sectarian violence and divisions from the 1960s to the 1990s.

ABOVE:
OSCAR WILDE
The successful playwright and novelist is also known for his convictions for gross indecency and homosexual acts, which have reverberated down the generations in the gay rights movement and wider society. He was imprisoned but received a posthumous pardon from the UK government in 2017.

OPPOSITE:
PHIL LYNOTT
Born in the English West Midlands to an Irish mother and a father from British Guiana, Phil Lynott was raised by his mother's parents in Dublin. There he formed Thin Lizzy, which had a number of international hits in the 1970s.

Modern Ireland has also become a place with its own film industry. Apart from international hits set in Ireland such as *The Commitments*, *Angela's Ashes* and *My Left Foot*, both the Republic and Northern Ireland have provided many a backdrop for factual or fictional tales. Ballinesker Beach in County Wexford doubled up as D-Day's Omaha Beach for the opening scene of *Saving Private Ryan*; the island of Skellig Michael was used as Luke

TAMA

THE POGUES

The late Shane MacGowan (right), and Spider Stacy of The Pogues pictured just before the release of their Christmas hit 'Fairytale of New York' – a duet with Kirsty MacColl – in 1987. Formed in London, the band popularised Irish music by fusing it with punk.

MARCH 17, 1987
THE POGUES

LEFT & ABOVE:
GEORGIAN DUBLIN
Ireland has many sights to see and tourism has become a major part of its economy, particularly in Dublin. Those going to Dublin Castle can see the 1761-built Bedford Tower (left). The Irish Crown Jewels were stolen from here in 1907.

Dublin experienced a growth spurt as a city in the eighteenth and nineteenth centuries and – unlike its British counterparts – did not suffer bombing in World War II because Ireland was neutral. As a result, much of its fine Georgian architecture is preserved, such as Mount Street Upper (pictured above).

Skywalker's home in two of the twenty-first century's *Star Wars* films; and *Game of Thrones* episodes have been filmed in many locations around Northern Ireland.

Some of the best-loved television shows of recent years have also come out of Ireland – for instance, *Father Ted*, *Derry Girls* and *Ballykissangel*.

SPORTING SUCCESS

Ireland has also had international success at sport, with its rugby team's successive Six Nations titles in recent years and the Republic's football team, under Jack Charlton in the 1980s and 1990s, beating the likes of England in a European Championship and Italy in a World Cup. Tellingly, the make-up of Charlton's sides contained players brought up in England and Scotland, who qualified to play for Ireland

GUINNESS BREWERY
Guinness's Brewery in Dublin is a sightseeing venue as well as where the brand's famous stout is created. However, the Guinness family history is at odds with a product that is such an Irish icon. The founder of the beer, Arthur Guinness, was a devout Protestant and in later generations the family was also steadfast in its loyalty to the Crown.

ESTD 1759
GUINNESS™
ST JAMES'S GATE
DUBLIN, IRELA

TEMPLE BAR

Temple Bar, on the south side of the River Liffey in Dublin, is promoted as a cultural destination in the city, and the streets there are lined with bars and pubs. Much favoured by people on city breaks to Dublin, it contains one venue specifically called The Temple Bar pub – although the name Temple Bar refers to the whole network of streets and squares.

THE
TEMPLE BAR
Traditional
Irish Music
TEMPLE
BAR
Estb. 1840
EMPERO
MALTED LIQUO
GUINNES
traditional
irish
Restaurant

because they had parents or grandparents who had emigrated.

Modernisation in Ireland went hand in hand with it joining the European Economic Community (EEC) in 1973, at the same time as the United Kingdom did. However, the Republic has not had the fractious relationship with Europe that Britain has and remains a part of the European Union (EU), and adopted its currency, the euro, in 2002. As investment poured into the Republic, an economic boom started, known as the Celtic Tiger, transforming Ireland into one of Europe's wealthiest countries. Despite a severe economic downturn following the financial crisis of 2008, today, Ireland's economy remains healthy, with a strong labour market.

A CHANGING SOCIETY

As in the Republic, church-going has been falling in the twenty-first century in Northern Ireland, reflecting the drops in numbers of people in pews across the Western world. And as this has happened, so the assumption that virtually all Catholics in Northern Ireland would be in favour of a united Ireland has been questioned, along with the belief that Protestants would want to stay in Britain, which has left the EU.

Whatever happens, the legacies left by the invasion of the English, and the settlement of large numbers of Scots in Northern Ireland, are still writ large across the island in the twenty-first century. However modern both the Republic and Northern Ireland are now, with much of their economies service-based, and with equal rights across the board, the conflicted history of the Emerald Isle remains.

WEST COAST BEAUTY

Skellig Michael, with its peaks and early Christian monastery, is one of the draws of Ireland's wild west coast. The counties of Cork, Kerry and Galway are popular destinations for those seeking the striking scenery of the western fringe of Ireland, with its rocky peninsulas, uninhabited islands and now-marooned monasteries.

SIX NATIONS WINNERS
As well as Ireland having an oversized influence on world culture, it has also punched above its weight in certain sports. In recent years its rugby union team has tasted great success in the Six Nations, with Ireland winning the tournament six times since 2009. Here centre Gordon Darcy carries against Wales during a triumphant 2009 Six Nations campaign.

canterbury

SEAMUS HEANEY

Seamus Heaney was a much-lauded poet from near Lough Neagh in Northern Ireland. He began publishing poems in the 1960s, to much critical acclaim. In 1995 he received the Nobel Prize in Literature. He was a professor at Harvard from 1981 to 1997 and was their Poet in Residence from 1988 to 2006. He died in 2013.

Picture Credits

Alamy: 6 (David Lyons), 8/9 (PA Images), 10 top (RM Ireland), 12/13 (Holmes Garden Photos), 14/15 top (George Munday), 15 bottom (scenicireland.com), 20 (Rik Hamilton), 21 (David Lyons), 22 bottom (Lebrecht Music & Arts), 26/27 (Joana Kruse), 30/31 (Connect Images), 32 (Hemis), 34/35 (aphperspective), 36 (Colin Underhill), 37 (CPA Media Pte Ltd), 40 (David Taylor Photography), 43 (Steve Vidler), 44 top (Paolo Romiti), 44 bottom (Penta Springs Limited), 46/47 (Sryan Bruen), 48/49 (scenicireland.com), 52 (Chronicle), 53 top (Dorling Kindersley ltd), 53 bottom (Homer Sykes), 56/57 (Album), 58 (imageBroker.com), 60 (Classic Image), 66/67 (Albert Knapp), 68 top (The Granger Collection), 69 (De Luan), 72 (Chronicle), 73 (Art Directors & Trip), 76 (Reading Room 2020), 78 (Barry Mason), 83 (Historical Image Archive), 86 (The History Emporium), 89 (Classic Image), 92 (Historical Image Archive), 95 (Ognyan Yosifov), 96/97 (Stephen Barnes IE), 100 (Science History Images), 104/105 (Penta Springs Limited), 106 (Chronicle), 110 bottom (Pictorial Press Ltd), 111 (Maurice Savage), 112 (Chronicle), 113 (Eye Ubiquitous), 116 (travelib history), 123 (Nigel Cattlin), 124/125 (De Luan), 126 (World History Archive), 132 (Lebrecht Music & Arts), 135 (Pictorial Press Ltd), 137 (Classic Image), 138/139 (Historical Image Archive), 140 (M&N), 145 (Pictorial Press Ltd), 148 (The Reading Room), 151 (Historical Image Archive), 154/155 (De Luan), 156/157 (PA Images), 160/161 (InterFoto), 162 (Chronicle), 163 (Chris Bull), 171 (De Luan), 174/175 (Associated Press), 176/177 (Shawn Williams), 198 (PA Images), 199 (Trinity Mirror), 200/201 (Associated Press), 205 (meanderingemu), 206/207 (Pictorial Press Ltd), 210/211 (Stephen Parker), 218/219 (David Lyons), 220/221 (PA Images)

Creative Commons Attribution-Share Alike 2.0 Generic license: 209 (Harry Potts)

Creative Commons Attribution-Share Alike 4.0 International license: 33 (Andreas F. Borchert)

Creative Commons Attribution-Share Alike 4.0 International license: 24 (Sheila1988), 149 (National Gallery of Ireland)

Dreamstime: 11 (Gabe9000c), 19 top (Yullika), 28 (MNStudio), 50/51 (MNStudio), 212/213 (Gazzag), 213 (Tupungato), 214/215 (4kclips), 216/217 (Attila Tatár)

Getty Images: 22 top (Ashmolean Museum), 61 (Heritage Images), 64 (The Print Collector), 68 bottom (CM Dixon), 82 (Universal History Archive), 87 (Fine Art Images), 94 & 98 (Hulton Archive), 108/109 (Universal History Archive), 114 (HUM Images), 128/129 (Keystone France), 130 (fpg), 131 (Bettmann), 142/143 (Heritage Images), 144 (Ivy Close Images), 152 top & 158/159 (Central Press), 164/165 (Daily Mirror), 166/167 (fpg), 168/169 (Hulton Deutsch), 172/173 (Topical Press Agency), 178 (David Soanes Photography), 182 (Davis), 183 top (Central Press), 183 bottom (Keystone), 184/185 (Hulton Deutsch), 186 (Independent Newspapers Ireland), 187 (John Cogil), 188/189 (Alex Bowie), 190/191 (Stan Meagher), 192 (A. Jones), 193 top (Keystone), 193 bottom (Sean Meagher), 194/195 (Alex Bowie), 196/197 (William L. Rukeyser), 202/203 (robert wallis), 222/223 (Colin McPherson)

iStock: 45 (mammuth)

National Museum of Ireland: 14 bottom

Public Domain: 51 (Claíomh Solais), 70/71 (Blight55), 77 (PKM), 80/81 (Skibly113), 88 (Hohum), 90/91 (Eastfarthingan), 93 (Dcoetzee), 99 (Soerfm), 101 (Dcoetzee), 102/103 (Scolaire), 107 (Fæ), 110 top (Thespoondragon), 115 (Dcoetzee), 118 (Chris 73), 119 (fdrmrzusa), 122 (Neveselbert), 127 (PastelLilac), 134, 136, 141 (Library of Congress), 150 (Holly Cheng), 152 bottom (Gradinari), 153 (WD Hogan), 170 (National Library of Ireland on The Commons), 204, 208 (Docu), 146/147 (National Library of Ireland)

Public Record Office of Northern Ireland: 180/181

Shutterstock: 5 (Jrossphoto), 10 bottom (makasana photo), 16/17 (pgaborphotos), 19 bottom (Hanging Bear Media), 23 top (Michalakis Ppalis), 23 bottom (Remizov), 38/39 (Kevin George), 42 (VanderWolf Images), 54/55 (ianmitchinson), 62/63 (agaglowala), 65 (Pavel Voitukovic), 74/75 (Mike Drosos), 84/85 (MNStudio), 120/121 (Giannis Papanikos)